Introduction

This Teacher's Resource Book contains thirty-one photocopiable activities and further ideas for you to use with *New Headway Intermediate*. It is a new component for the *Headway* series and has been written with two aims in mind:

- to give teachers additional material that revises and extends the work in the Student's Book

- to give students lots of extra speaking practice!

Students at intermediate level need lots of vocabulary and grammar input. Controlled skills work is also important to develop their reading, writing, listening, and speaking. But at the same time, it is also essential that they are given opportunities to 'get active' and actually use their English in meaningful and relevant contexts.

The activities in this book are designed to help your students do this. They encourage students to talk about themselves, compare opinions and views about the world, and practise the kind of situations they are likely to encounter in real life.

In addition, every activity involves an element of team work. Students work together to share or check information, and agree outcomes or solutions. In other words, every activity encourages purposeful interaction where students need to speak and listen to each other.

Through role plays, language games, questionnaires, and information-gap activities, students are also given the chance to build their confidence and introduce a more personal dimension to their learning.

How to use the photocopiable activities

Each activity starts with the following information:

Aim	The main focus of the activity
Language	The grammar/function exploited
Skills	Speaking, Reading, Writing, and/or Listening
Lesson link	Suggestion for when to use the worksheet
Materials	Notes for preparation of worksheet

Pre-activity

These activities act as a warm-up before students carry out the main activity. They act to remind students of the necessary language needed and to set the context. They are optional, particularly if following straight on from the lesson in the Student's Book.

Procedure

This section has step-by-step instructions for carrying out the main activity. Each main activity takes between fifteen and thirty minutes and is suitable for most class sizes. (There are additional notes for larger classes.) For each activity there is a photocopiable worksheet. Some of the worksheets need to be cut up before handing out to students.

Extension

After each main activity, there is a suggestion for an extension activity. These are generally writing activities which build on the language or topics covered in the main activity. They can be assigned for homework.

Contents

Worksheet	Description	Language
7.1 Get that job!	Interviewing and selecting candidates for four jobs	Present Perfect Simple; Past Simple
7.2 Snap!	Matching passive sentences to their active equivalent	Active and Passive
7.3 Talk about yourself	Asking and discussing questions about personal experience	Multi-word verbs, e.g. *put up with*, *take after*, *go out with*; Question forms
8.1 Future scope	Discussing possible future inventions	Second conditional
8.2 Strong adjectives crossword	Completing a crossword by exchanging definitions for strong adjectives	Strong adjectives, e.g. *hilarious*, *enormous*
9.1 Out of context	Discussing what a person is doing from his facial expression, gestures and posture	Modal verbs of probability in the present, e.g. *must*, *could*, *might*, *can't*
9.2 Whodunnit?	Deducing from clues who is most likely to have committed a crime	Modal verbs of probability in the past
10.1 Compound noun competition	Matching cards to make compound nouns	Compound nouns
10.2 Holiday blues	Role playing complaining about a hotel and some guests	Complaining
11.1 Kidnapped!	Role playing a press conference	Indirect questions
11.2 It's easy, isn't it?	Matching statements with question tags	Question tags; Intonation
11.3 In my opinion	Taking part in a debate	Presenting opinions
12.1 The bugged conversation	Preparing a radio report about a conversation between two criminals	Reported speech Reporting verbs, e.g. *beg, warn*
12.2 I'm really sorry!	Role playing situations where an apology is required	Apologizing and explaining

1.1

Aim	
To introduce a guest on a chat show	
Language	
Questions	
Fluency practice	
Skills	
Speaking	
Lesson link	
Use after Unit 1, SB p9	
Materials	
One copy of the worksheet cut in half per pair of students	

Pre-activity (5 minutes)

- Ask students to imagine they are going to interview a famous person. Brainstorm questions they would ask him/her, e.g. *Where are you from? When did you start acting? Who inspired you to start writing? What are your plans for this year?* etc.

Procedure (20 minutes)

- Explain that students are chat show hosts and that they have invited another student to appear on their show. First they are going to interview the student to find out some background information. Then they are going to introduce him/her to the audience on their chat show.

- Divide students into pairs and give each student a copy of the worksheet. Give students time to think of the questions they would need to ask to complete the interview card.

- Students interview each other and note the answers on the interview card. Go around listening, helping and correcting as necessary.

- When everybody is ready, group two pairs together to make groups of four students. Students take it in turns to be the chat show host and introduce their partner to the audience (the other pair in the group) using the notes they have made. Go around listening, noting down any common errors to go over at the end.

Extension (5 minutes)

- Display all the interview cards on the classroom wall. Allow students time to read them and find out about each other.

Name _____

Birthday _____

Family _____

Job _____

Language spoken _____

Hobbies and interests _____

_____

Likes _____

Dislikes _____

Places visited _____

A memorable event in your past _____

_____

Something you'd really like to do _____

_____

Something you plan to do soon _____

_____

✂ --

Name _____

Birthday _____

Family _____

Job _____

Language spoken _____

Hobbies and interests _____

_____

Likes _____

Dislikes _____

Places visited _____

A memorable event in your past _____

_____

Something you'd really like to do _____

_____

Something you plan to do soon _____

_____

1.2

Nice to meet you!

Aim		
To practise keeping a conversation going		
Language		
Questions		
Tense review		
Question tags		
Skills		
Speaking		
Lesson link		
Use after Unit 1, SB p9		
Materials		
One copy of the worksheet cut up per group of four to six students		

Pre-activity (10 minutes)

- Write the following jumbled conversation the board:

	Steffi:	Just over five years. How about you?
a	Frank:	We met on holiday in Africa.
	Steffi:	Hi, you're Frank, aren't you? I'm Steffi.
b	Frank:	Nice to meet you. How do you know Annie?
	Steffi:	Anyway, nice to meet you, Frank.
c	Frank:	Nice to meet you, too.
	Steffi:	How interesting!
d	Frank:	Yes, and we've stayed in touch ever since.
	Steffi:	We're colleagues. Actually, she's my boss.
e	Frank:	Oh really? How long have you known her?

- Explain that Steffi and Frank are at Annie's party. Ask students, in pairs, to put the conversation in the correct order. Then check the order with the class (b, e, a, d, c).

- Ask students to look at the conversation and find phrases that Steffi and Frank use to keep the conversation going, e.g. *aren't you? How about you? How interesting! Oh, really?*

- Work though the dialogue with the class drilling stress and intonation. Then ask students, in pairs, to practise the dialogue.

Procedure (20 minutes)

- Explain that students are at a party with people they have never met before. The host is their friend, Mikhail Pellman, who is a famous film director. He has invited all his friends from around the world to help him celebrate winning an Oscar for his latest film, *Streets*. Students are going to talk to each other at the party and try to keep each conversation going for as as long as possible.

- Divide students into groups of four to six and give each student a different role card. Give students time to check any items of vocabulary and to memorize the information on the card.

- In their groups, students mingle and have conversations with everybody at the party. Go around listening, helping as necessary and noting any common errors to go over at the end.

- Have a class feedback session. Ask students to tell you what they found about each other and how successful they were at keeping their conversations going.

Extension (15 minutes)

- Ask students, on their own, to write down (and if necessary develop) a conversation they had at the party, using phrases to keep the conversation going. Go around helping as necessary.

Lionel/Lynn

Age:	52
Birthplace:	Philadelphia
Nationality:	American
Lives:	New York
Status:	Single (but you have a girlfriend/boyfriend)
Profession:	Film editor

You've known Mikhail for nearly thirty years! You went to film school together and you've worked together on several film productions.

Clive/Claire

Age:	25
Birthplace:	Sydney
Nationality:	Australian
Lives:	Los Angeles
Status:	Single
Profession:	Actor

You were the leading actor in Mikhail's film, *Streets*. This was the first time you've worked together. In fact, this is the first film you've ever done!

Mario/Maria

Age:	42
Birthplace:	Milan
Nationality:	Italy
Lives:	Paris
Status:	Married
Profession:	Journalist

You became friends with Mikhail eight years ago after you interviewed him for your newspaper. You both love good food and wine so there's always a lot to talk about!

George/Georgia

Age:	32
Birthplace:	Montreal
Nationality:	Irish
Lives:	Dublin
Status:	Married with one son
Profession:	Doctor

You're Mikhail's personal doctor. You travel with him everywhere because he needs close medical attention. Next week you're both going to Moscow to start a new film. It's your first time there!

Péter/Petra

Age:	75
Birthplace:	Budapest
Nationality:	Hungarian
Lives:	London
Status:	Widowed with two daughters
Profession:	Retired film director

Mikhail came to work with you when he left film school. That was thirty years ago! You didn't work with each other for long but you've always stayed in touch.

Julian/Julia

Age:	21
Birthplace:	Taipei
Nationality:	Taiwanese
Lives:	Hong Kong
Status:	Single
Profession:	Student

You're best friends with Mikhail's daughter. You've never met him before this party, but he still paid for your flight. He's so generous!

1.3

The sound of murder!

Aim

To solve a murder using phonetic symbols

Language

Phonetics

Pronunciation

Skills

Speaking

Lesson link

Use after Unit 1, SB p12

Materials

One copy of the worksheet per pair of students

Answers

1 /m/	7 /z/
2 /eə/	8 /ə/
3 /r/	9 /n/
4 /ɪ/	10 /d/
5 /p/	11 /aɪ/
6 /ɔɪ/	

Murderer:	Mary /ˈmeərɪ/
Murder weapon:	poison /ˈpɔɪzən/
Object taken:	diamond /ˈdaɪəmənd/

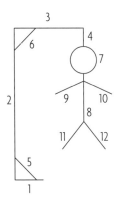

Pre-activity (5 minutes)

- Write the following countries on the board in phonetic script: /dʒəˈpæn/ (Japan), /ˈɪtəli/ (Italy), /ˈpəʊlənd/ (Poland), /ˌɑːdʒənˈtiːnə/ (Argentina), /ˈɪndiə/ (India).

- Divide students into pairs. Give them one minute to decipher the phonetic script to find the countries. (There's a table of phonetic symbols at the back of the Student's Book.)

Procedure (20 minutes)

- Explain that students are going to use phonetic symbols to solve a murder. Tell students the details of the crime and check that everyone understands: *The famous rock star, Kurt Studman, has been killed. A coded message was sent to the local police station. When the code is broken it reveals details about the name of the murderer, the murder weapon, and an object which was taken.*

- Divide students into pairs and give each pair a copy of the worksheet. (If you have an uneven number of students, make one group of three students.) Ask students to read the message which was sent to the police station and identify the eleven sounds that are numbered in the message. Go around helping as necessary.

- Tell students, in their pairs, to decide which phonetic symbol represents each sound 1–11 and then write the phonetic symbol in the *Code breaker* boxes below the message. Go around checking and helping as necessary.

- When students have completed the *Code breaker* boxes, ask them to sound out the words to work out the answer for each item (murderer, murder weapon, and object taken). You can make this game competitive by setting a time limit of ten minutes.

- Have a class feedback session to check the answers.

Extension (15 minutes)

- Play *Hangman* using phonetic symbols instead of letters. Think of a word, e.g. computer (/kəmˈpjuːtə/) and write a dash on the board for each of the eight symbols. Students try to guess the word by calling out sounds at random. Write in any correct sounds. Each wrong sound called out makes up one line of the hangman picture (of which there are twelve). The class wins the game if they guess the word before you have finished the picture.

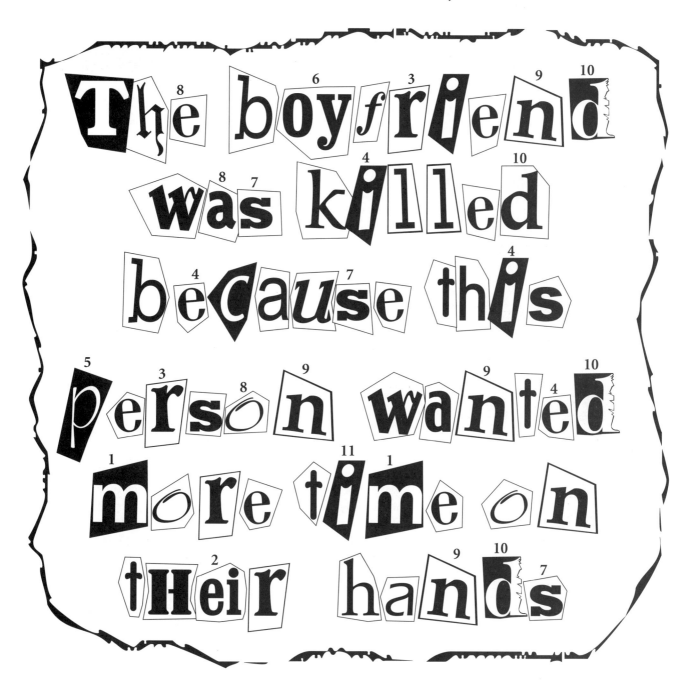

CODE BREAKER

Write the phonetic symbol for each sound under the numbers to solve the murder.

		1	2	3	4		
Murderer:							
		5	6	7	8	9	
Murder weapon:							
		10	11	1	8	9	10
Object taken:							

2.1

Aim
To devise a questionnaire to assess happiness

Language
Present Simple
Fluency practice

Skills
Speaking and Writing

Lesson link
Use after Unit 2, SB p15

Materials
One copy of the worksheet per student

Score box

0–10	extremely happy
11–20	happy
21–30	not very happy
31–40	unhappy

Pre-activity (5 minutes)

- Divide students into small groups and ask them to think of five things which are important for happiness, e.g. *good friends, interesting job, enough money,* etc.

- Have a class feedback session to compare ideas.

Procedure (20 minutes)

- Explain that students are going to make a questionnaire to assess how happy they really are.

- Divide students into pairs and give each student a copy of the worksheet. Make sure everybody understands the categories.

- Ask students, in their pairs, to write a positive statement for each category on the worksheet, e.g. *I'm happiest when I live on my own* (Home life). *I like working in a team* (Professional life), etc. Explain that students don't necessarily have to agree with the statements they write.

- When everybody has finished, pair students with a different partner. Students take it in turns to interview each other. Student A reads out his/her statement for each category and Student B gives the statement a mark from 1 to 5 depending on how strongly he/she agrees with it (5 = strongly agrees, 1 = strongly disagrees). Student A notes Student B's marks in the first box by each statement. Then Student B reads out his/her statements for Student A to give a mark.

- Then Student A reads his/her statements for a second time and Student B gives the statements a mark from 1 to 5 depending on how closely the statement reflects his/her own life (5 = reflects exactly, 1 = doesn't reflect at all). Student A notes Student B's marks in the second box by each statement. Then Student B reads his/her statements for Student A to give a mark.

- Now students calculate their partner's happiness score by looking at the difference between the two sets of marks in each category, e.g. a student who recorded 5 and then 1 for a category would have a happiness rating of 4.

- Have a class feedback session. Write the score box on the board. Ask students if they agree!

Extension (10 minutes)

- Working in small groups, students rank the categories on the worksheet according to which they think affect happiness the most. Encourage your students to argue their case if there are differences of opinion. Then have a class feedback session.

How happy are you?

		Agree/Disagree	Is it true for you?
Home life		☐	☐
Social life		☐	☐
Professional life		☐	☐
Family life		☐	☐
Financial life		☐	☐
Love life		☐	☐
Intellectual life		☐	☐
Holiday life		☐	☐

Statement

2.2

Let's talk sport!

Aim

To play a board game to talk about and answer questions about sport

Language

Sports vocabulary

Fluency practice

Skills

Speaking and Listening

Lesson link

Use after Unit 2, SB p22

Materials

One copy of the board and the cards cut up per group of four students. Each group will need a coin and each student will need a counter

Pre-activity (10 minutes)

- Brainstorm sports vocabulary with the class by asking questions, e.g. *Which sports need a ball? (football, volleyball, basketball) a racket? (tennis, badminton, squash). How many players are there in a football team? (eleven) a basketball team? (five). In which sports do you score goals? (football) points? (squash, volleyball, badminton),* etc.

- Divide students into pairs. Ask students to take it in turns to describe a sport for their partner to guess. Go around listening, helping and correcting as necessary.

Procedure (30 minutes)

- Explain that students are going to play a board game about sport.

- Divide students into groups of four, two teams of two students. Give each group a copy of the board game and a set of *Quiz* cards, *Sixty seconds* cards, and *Which sport?* cards placed face down in three piles on the table.

- Explain that teams take it in turns to toss a coin to move around the board (heads = move one square, tails = move two squares). Students will land on three different squares:

  Quiz a student from the opposing team asks the playing team a general knowledge question

  Sixty seconds a student talks about a subject for sixty seconds

  Which sport? a student describes a sport (without saying the sport) for his/her partner to guess

  If a team successfully complete a task, they can move forward from that square next turn. If the task is not completed successfully, the team go back one square.

- Go around listening while students are playing, helping and correcting as necessary, and making sure that students in each team share the speaking activities. You may like to note down any common errors to go over at the end.

- The team in each group to finish first wins.

Extension (20 minutes)

- Ask students to prepare a public information advert to promote playing a team sport as a way of keeping fit. Go around helping with vocabulary as necessary.

- When everybody has finished, display the adverts on the classroom wall. Give students time to read each other's work.

QUIZ
Q How many players are there in an ice-hockey team?
A Five.

QUIZ
Q Where were the 2000 Olympics held?
A Sydney, Australia.

Sixty seconds

A sport you would like to learn

QUIZ
Q Where does Sumo wrestling come from?
A Japan.

QUIZ
Q What is the top mark a judge can award in ice-skating?
A Six.

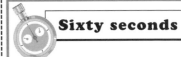
Sixty seconds

A sport that any age group can play

QUIZ
Q How many points do you need to win a game of volleyball?
A Fifteen.

QUIZ
Q In tennis, what does '15–Love' mean?
A Fifteen points versus zero points.

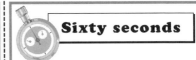
Sixty seconds

A dangerous sport

QUIZ
Q What are the colours of the referee's shirt in most American sports?
A Black and white.

QUIZ
Q Which is an extreme sport: bungee jumping, horse riding, or aerobics?
A Bungee jumping.

Sixty seconds

A sport you like to watch

QUIZ
Q In baseball, how many chances do you get to hit the ball?
A Three.

QUIZ
Q In which country does the football team Lazio play?
A Italy.

Sixty seconds

A sport you hate

QUIZ
Q In which sport do you use a shuttlecock: badminton or fishing?
A Badminton.

QUIZ
Q Which is harder: a tennis ball or a cricket ball?
A A cricket ball.

Sixty seconds

An extreme sport, e.g. parachuting, you would/wouldn't like to try

Sixty seconds **Which do you prefer: team or individual sports?**		
 **Sixty seconds** **A sport you think should be banned**		
Sixty seconds **A popular sport in your country**		
Sixty seconds **A sport you like to play**		
Sixty seconds **A sport you used to play as a child**		
Sixty seconds **A sport that requires speed and agility**		

3.1

Aim

To create an imaginary life story using prompts

Language

Past Simple

Time phrases, e.g. *when, while, during*

Emotions vocabulary

Skills

Speaking and Writing

Lesson link

Use after Unit 3, SB p26

Materials

One copy of the worksheet per student

Pre-activity (5 minutes)

- Write these words on the board: *childhood, teenage years, young adult, middle age,* and *old age.* Ask students to tell you the approximate time scales of each life stage.

Procedure (25 minutes)

- Explain that students are going to create an imaginary life story about a woman called Jane Harris.

- Divide students into pairs and give each student a copy of the worksheet. Read the introductory paragraph with the class. Then ask students to look at the emotions she felt in her life. Explain any unfamiliar words.

- Ask students, in their pairs, to invent a persona for Jane Harris. If necessary, ask questions to prompt them, e.g. *What kind of person was she? What did she do?* etc. Then ask them to imagine what happened to her, the places she went to, and the people she met during each of her life stages, linking each event to an emotion on the worksheet. Go around helping with vocabulary as necessary.

- Explain that students are now going to talk with a new partner about Jane's life.

- Reorganize students into new pairs. Students now compare the lives they have created. Encourage students to use the time phrases *when, while,* and *during* to make the story flow more smoothly. Go around listening, helping and correcting as necessary.

- Have a class feedback session. Ask individual students to tell you an event from their new partner's account of Jane's life and the emotion she felt.

Extension (15 minutes)

- In their original pairs, ask students to choose one of the life stages and write a diary entry for Jane. Go around helping as necessary.

Jane Harris ... an ordinary life?

Jane Harris was born in 1930. When she was a child she lived with her parents in a small village in the north of England. During her life there were good times, but there were also bad times. Here are some of the emotions she felt:

She felt successful.

She was uncertain.

She was afraid.

She felt free.

She was depressed.

She felt proud.

She felt in control.

She felt confident.

She was sad.

She felt trapped.

She was interested.

She was in love.

She was loved.

She felt lonely.

She felt secure.

She was excited.

She felt invisible.

She felt hopeless.

She was bored.

She was desperate.

She was happy.

She felt respected.

She grew tired.

She was angry.

Work with your partner to create Jane Harris' life story. Think about the different stages of her life: *childhood, teenage years, young adult, middle age,* and *old age.* Think about what happened in her life, the places she went to, and the people she met. Which emotions did she feel, and why?

3.2

Aim

To complete a crossword by asking for and giving definitions of words related to the arts

Language

Arts vocabulary, e.g. *painter, poem, fiction*

Skills

Speaking and Listening

Lesson link

Use after Unit 3, SB p29

Materials

One copy of the worksheet cut in half per pair of students

Pre-activity (5 minutes)

- Introduce the topic of the arts by asking students: *What's your favourite musical instrument? What kind of books do you enjoy reading the most? Which painter, musician, or writer (alive or dead) would you most like to meet? Why?* etc.

Procedure (20 minutes)

- Explain that students are going to work in pairs to complete an arts crossword puzzle. Students are going to take it in turns to give definitions to their partner.

- Divide students into pairs. Give Students A worksheet A, and Students B worksheet B. Tell students not to show each other their crosswords.

- Give students time to prepare their definitions. Encourage students to define the word as clearly as possible to help their partner but remind them that they cannot use the word in their definitions. Go around helping with vocabulary as necessary. (You may like to put students into AA and BB pairs during this preparation stage.)

- Students then complete the crossword by asking and answering, e.g. *What's number three? It's a drawing that you do very quickly.* Go around listening, helping and correcting as necessary.

- Tell students that they can check their answers because the letters in the shaded boxes make a type of book (*detective story*).

Extension (15 minutes)

- In groups of three or four, students write six general knowledge questions about the arts to test another group. Encourage students to write questions about art, music, and literature. Go around helping with vocabulary as necessary.

- Pair two groups together to ask each other the questions.

A

1. B A N D
2.
3. S K E T C H
4.
5. O R C H E S T R A
6.
7. P A I N T E R
8.
9. P O E M
10.
11. I N S T R U M E N T
12.
13. D R A W I N G
14.

✂ -

B

1.
2. C H A P T E R
3.
4. P A L E T T E
5.
6. A U T H O R
7.
8. N O V E L
9.
10. B R U S H
11.
12. F I C T I O N
13.
14. P L A Y

Photocopiable

3.3

Radio arts

Aim

To role play being arts critics discussing films and novels

Language

Expressing opinions

Skills

Writing, Speaking, and Listening

Lesson link

Use after Unit 3, SB p34

Materials

One copy of the worksheet cut in half per pair of students

Pre-activity (5 minutes)

- Write the following words on the board: *chapter, scene, plot, actor, character, author, director, novel, tension.* Ask students, in pairs, to decide which words can be used to talk about books (*chapter, author, novel*), which refer to films (*scene, actor, director*) and which can be used to talk about both (*plot, character, tension*).

- Have a class feedback session and explain any unfamiliar vocabulary.

Procedure (30 minutes)

- Explain that students are arts critics who are going to appear on a radio programme to give their opinions on a novel or a film.

- Divide students into an even number of pairs. (If necessary, make two groups of three students.) Give Pairs A worksheet A, and Pairs B worksheet B. Give students time to look at the categories on their worksheets and to check any items of vocabulary.

- Ask Pairs A to think of a film they both know well, and Pairs B to think of a novel or short story. Students complete their worksheet with notes about the film or novel in preparation for talking about it.

- When students have finished, combine pairs to make groups of four (Pair A and Pair B). Give Pair A a blank worksheet B, and Pair B a blank worksheet A. Pair A start by talking about their film. Pair B listen and take notes on the blank worksheet, and then ask questions to find out more about the film/novel. Then Pair B talk about their novel while Pair A take notes. Go around listening, helping and correcting as necessary.

- Have a class feedback session. Invite pairs to tell the class about the film/novel described by the other pair in their group.

Extension (20 minutes)

- Ask students, in pairs, to write a newspaper review (150 words) of the novel or film they discussed. Go around helping with vocabulary as necessary.

- Display the reviews on the classroom wall and give students time to read each other's work.

A

TALKING PICTURES

Title: _____

Director: _____

Actors: _____

Type of film: _____

Main characters: _____

Summary of plot: _____

_____

_____

Good points: _____

_____

Bad points: _____

_____

Score: _____/10

✂ --

B

Talking Prose

Title: _____

~~Director:~~ AUTHOR _____

~~Actors:~~ _____

NOVEL/SHORT STORY
~~Type of film:~~ _____

Main characters: _____

Summary of plot: _____

_____

_____

Good points: _____

_____

Bad points: _____

_____

Score: _____/10

4.1

House sharer's contract

Aim

To negotiate a set of house rules with new flatmates

Language

Modal verbs of permission and obligation, e.g. *allowed to, have to, can*

Skills

Speaking

Lesson link

Use after Unit 4, SB p35

Materials

One copy of the worksheet cut up per group of four students

Pre-activity (10 minutes)

- Introduce the topic of living with other people to the class. Ask: *Who do you live with? Is there anything you find difficult about living with other people?* etc.

- Divide students into pairs. Give students three minutes to brainstorm advantages and disadvantages of living with others and living alone. Then have a class feedback session.

Procedure (20 minutes)

- Explain that students have just moved into a house with two or three people they don't know. Although the agency promises to match up like-minded people, they all seem very different! Their task is to agree a set of house rules to help everyone get along.

- Brainstorm possible problem areas, e.g. *housework, cooking, bathroom, TV, noise, smoking, visitors, food shopping, use of the telephone, bills*, and elicit some example rules for each, e.g. *We should wash the dishes every day. You aren't allowed to smoke in common areas*, etc.

- Divide students into groups of four and give each student a role card. Give students time to read their role card, check any items of vocabulary, and consider how their role will affect their needs and priorities in the house.

- In their groups, students introduce themselves to their new housemates. Then they say what their needs are. As a group students agree at least one rule for each of the problem areas suggested, e.g. *Everybody has to share the housework. People are allowed to play music, but they must be quiet after 10.30 p.m.* Go around listening, helping and correcting as necessary.

- Have a class feedback session to compare the rules established in each house. Ask students if they are happy with the outcome, or if there are rules they would find difficult to live with in their role.

Extension (15 minutes)

- Tell students that they have been living in the house for a month, but the other housemates have consistently broken the rules agreed at the beginning. Ask them, in pairs, to write a letter of complaint to the agency. Go around helping with vocabulary as necessary.

House SHARERS

We'll find you the right home and the right people!

Name:	Anna O'Donnell
Age:	20
Occupation:	University student
Disposable income:	£50 a week
Status:	Single (with lots of friends!)
Are you a smoker?:	Yes – 20 a day
Interests/hobbies:	Dance music, cooking, playing the guitar, sleeping
Other comments:	I want to live with people who don't worry if the house gets a bit untidy. I like to stay up late. I'd like to use the house for parties from time to time.

House SHARERS

We'll find you the right home and the right people!

Name:	Gordon Lansdowne
Age:	27
Occupation:	Teacher
Disposable income:	£200 a week
Status:	Single with a girlfriend
Are you a smoker?:	No (I suffer from asthma)
Interests/hobbies:	Reading, watching silent movies
Other comments:	I hate mess and uncleanliness! I also have to prepare lessons in the evening and need some peace and quiet.

House SHARERS

We'll find you the right home and the right people!

Name:	Martin Grant
Age:	33
Occupation:	Butcher
Disposable income:	£100 a week
Status:	Divorced (my three-year-old son lives with my ex-partner)
Are you a smoker?:	Yes – in the evening
Interests/hobbies:	Watching football on the television, rebuilding old motorbikes
Other comments:	My son often comes to stay with me at weekends, so my housemates should like children.

House SHARERS

We'll find you the right home and the right people!

Name:	Charlotte Drake
Age:	25
Occupation:	Musician
Disposable income:	£180 a week
Status:	Single (my boyfriend lives in Australia)
Are you a smoker?:	No!
Interests/hobbies:	Painting, playing the trumpet
Other comments:	I'm a vegetarian and I would like to live with other people who are the same. I also need to phone my boyfriend at least once a week.

4.2

Are you right for the job?

Aim

To discuss personalities and suitability for a variety of jobs

Language

Adjectives of personality and behaviour, e.g. *easy-going, well-dressed*

Skills

Speaking and Listening

Lesson link

Use after Unit 4, SB p39

Materials

One copy of the worksheet cut up per six students

Pre-activity (5 minutes)

- Ask students to think about what kind of person would be best suited to a particular job, e.g. an ambulance driver. Ask: *What personal qualities should this person have?* (e.g. *reliable, caring, ability to stay calm under pressure*). Give your students two minutes to brainstorm their ideas in pairs. Then have a class feedback session.

Procedure (30 minutes)

- Explain that students are going to interview each other and then choose a job for their partner according to their personality.

- Divide students into pairs and give each student an adjective card. Ask students to interview each other about their personalities and circle the adjectives on their card which apply to their partner. Encourage students to explain why they think they have particular personality traits, e.g. *I think I am lazy because I don't like getting up in the morning. Once I stayed in bed all day!* Go around listening, helping and correcting as necessary.

- Give each student a job card. In their pairs, students discuss what kind of person would be best suited to each job and write the relevant adjectives on the back of the two job cards.

- When everybody has finished, ask students to find a job for their partner. Students mingle as a class and tell each other about the job they have and the kind of person they think would be best suited to it.

- Finally, students go back into their pairs and tell their partner which job they have chosen for them and why.

- Have a class feedback session to see if everyone is happy with the job their partner chose for them.

Extension (15 minutes)

- Ask students, in pairs, to write an advert for one of the jobs in the main activity, with particular emphasis on the kind of person they are looking for. Go around helping as necessary.

Adjective cards

hard-working easy-going punctual friendly reserved emotional lazy outgoing hospitable sociable formal casual enthusiastic quiet tolerant talkative sophisticated well-dressed fun-loving respectful humorous serious nationalistic romantic	hard-working easy-going punctual friendly reserved emotional lazy outgoing hospitable sociable formal casual enthusiastic quiet tolerant talkative sophisticated well-dressed fun-loving respectful humorous serious nationalistic romantic
hard-working easy-going punctual friendly reserved emotional lazy outgoing hospitable sociable formal casual enthusiastic quiet tolerant talkative sophisticated well-dressed fun-loving respectful humorous serious nationalistic romantic	hard-working easy-going punctual friendly reserved emotional lazy outgoing hospitable sociable formal casual enthusiastic quiet tolerant talkative sophisticated well-dressed fun-loving respectful humorous serious nationalistic romantic
hard-working easy-going punctual friendly reserved emotional lazy outgoing hospitable sociable formal casual enthusiastic quiet tolerant talkative sophisticated well-dressed fun-loving respectful humorous serious nationalistic romantic	hard-working easy-going punctual friendly reserved emotional lazy outgoing hospitable sociable formal casual enthusiastic quiet tolerant talkative sophisticated well-dressed fun-loving respectful humorous serious nationalistic romantic

Poet

Hotel Manager

Prime Minister

Children's TV Presenter

Teacher

Secret Agent

4.3

Aim	
To play a quiz game about different cultures	
Language	
Modal verbs of obligation	
Skills	
Reading, Writing, Speaking, and Listening	
Lesson link	
Use after Unit 4, SB p40 & 41	
Materials	
One copy of the worksheet cut into cards per four students	

Pre-activity (5 minutes)

• Introduce the topic of traditions and customs by asking students to describe what they do on the following days: *their birthday, a national holiday, New Year's Day,* etc. Do they have any customs which are special to their country or region?

Procedure (30 minutes)

• Explain that students are going to play a game where they guess the customs of different countries around the world. Show students how the game works by writing on the board: *In China you should greet someone a) by shaking his/her hand, b) with a nod and a bow, c) with a kiss on the cheeks.* Ask: *Which custom is the correct one?* (b).

• Divide students into four teams. (If you have a large class, divide students into eight teams.) Give Team A worksheet A, Team B worksheet B, and so on. Give students time to read the worksheet and to check any items of vocabulary.

• Tell students, in their groups, to brainstorm two incorrect answers for each question, as in the example on the board. Encourage them, if possible, to invent reasons to support their statements. Go around helping with vocabulary as necessary.

• When everybody has finished, pair two teams with different worksheets together to play the game. Sitting opposite each other, teams take it in turns to read out the custom and the three possible answers. The students in the other team discuss and choose which answer they think is correct. The team can bet 1, 2, or 3 points on their chosen answer depending on how confident they are that it is correct. If they answer correctly, they keep the points. If they answer incorrectly, they lose the points. Go around listening, helping and correcting as necessary.

• The team with the most points at the end wins.

• Have a class feedback session. Were your students surprised about any of the customs?

Extension (15 minutes)

• Ask students to write a leaflet to be given to visitors to their country when they arrive at the airport. Tell students that the leaflet should include five important customs or ways of behaving that will be useful to people who are visiting for the first time. Go around helping with vocabulary as necessary.

• Display all the leaflets on the classroom wall and give students time to read each other's work.

A *Call my cultural bluff*

1 In Britain, you don't have to carry:

   a _____

   b an identity card.

   c _____

2 In China, you shouldn't give a person:

   a white flowers (they are a symbol of tears and death).

   b _____

   c _____

3 If you are in a public place in Japan, you shouldn't:

   a _____

   b blow your nose.

   c _____

4 At Christmas, the French make a cake that contains a small porcelain doll. If the doll is in your slice of cake:

   a _____

   b _____

   c you are the king or queen for the evening, and you wear a crown.

B *Call my cultural bluff*

1 In Israel, you should never eat the following foods together:

   a meat and cheese (for religious reasons).

   b _____

   c _____

2 In India, you shouldn't point with your:

   a _____

   b feet.

   c _____

3 If you are in a restaurant in the United States, you should always add the following tip to your bill:

   a _____

   b _____

   c ten to fifteen per cent.

4 In Thailand, you shouldn't touch people on:

   a the head (the top of the head is considered to be sacred).

   b _____

   c _____

C *Call my cultural bluff*

1 If you are in somebody's home in Saudi Arabia you should never say how much you like things you see because:

   a _____

   b _____

   c The host will feel obliged to give them to you.

2 When you enter a home in Finland, you should:

   a _____

   b take off your shoes.

   c _____

3 Body language in Turkey is sometimes very different. For example:

   a a nod means "no" and a shake of the head means "yes".

   b _____

   c _____

4 If you are invited to somebody's home in the Philippines, it is a custom to bring:

   a a gift from your town or region.

   b _____

   c _____

D *Call my cultural bluff*

1 The British have a traditional dance where:

   a _____

   b the dancers wear bells, and a clown hits members of the audience with a ball.

   c _____

2 In Egypt, it is unacceptable to touch a person:

   a on the back of his/her neck.

   b _____

   c _____

3 The Spanish have a special way of celebrating midnight on New Year's Eve:

   a _____

   b _____

   c They eat twelve grapes as the clock chimes.

4 If you give flowers to someone in Germany, you should:

   a _____

   b buy an uneven number, and take them out of the wrapping paper first.

   c _____

5.1

Aim

To decide who is going to buy various items for a trip

Language

going to and *will*

Skills

Speaking and Listening

Lesson link

Use after Unit 5, SB p46 & 47

Materials

One copy of the worksheet cut into cards per group of four students

Answers

Student A

Bank: cash, Zanian dollars, traveller's cheques
Chemist: aspirin, mosquito repellent, first aid kit
Market: cheese, bread, bananas

Student B

Bus station: timetable, tickets to the airport, left-luggage information
Embassy: visa application, important info, UK embassy address
Post office: pens, writing paper, envelopes

Student C

Bookshop: maps, travel guides, dictionary
Camping shop: hiking boots, sleeping bag, rucksack
Travel agent: rail info, travel brochures, flight information

Student D

Supermarket: shampoo, soap, toothpaste
Photo shop: video camera, film, camera,
Radio/TV shop: portable radio, batteries, Walkman

Nobody has plans to go to the Doctor.

Pre-activity (5 minutes)

- Ask students to imagine they are going on an adventure holiday next week. In small groups, give students three minutes to brainstorm all the things they'd take with them, e.g. sleeping bag, torch, tent, maps, etc.

- Have a class feedback session.

Procedure (30 minutes)

- Explain that students are going on an adventure holiday to Zania (not a real country) and that they are preparing for the trip.

- Divide students into groups of four. Give Students A worksheet A, Students B worksheet B, and so on. Give students time to look at their worksheet and to check any items of vocabulary.

- Explain that each person in the group has a list of three places they plan to go to and a list of things they still need. Students, in their groups, discuss their plans and lists and decide who is going to do or get each thing. Each student should end up getting three things at each of the three places on their lists. There is one place which isn't on anyone's list but where they all need to go. Go around listening, helping and correcting as necessary.

- Have a class feedback session.

Extension (5 minutes)

- Ask students, in their groups, to discuss organizing trips or days away with friends. Do they find that the job of organizing everything is equally shared among everybody or is there always one person who ends up having to do all the work?

A

TRIP TO ZANIA

To do

Bank – cash

Chemist – aspirin

Market – cheese

Things we still need:

maps

film for camera

another sleeping bag

writing paper

travel brochures about Zania

bus timetable to airport

visa application forms for Zania

radio to listen to BBC World Service

shampoo

hepatitis injection

B

TRIP TO ZANIA

To do

Bus station – tickets to airport

Embassy – visa application

Post office – pens

Things we still need:

Zanian dollars

batteries for torch and radio

toothpaste

bread for the journey to the airport

travel guides about Zania

hiking boots

flight information for flights to Zania

aspirin

new camera

typhoid injection

C

TRIP TO ZANIA

To do

Bookshop – maps

Camping shop – hiking boots

Travel agent – railway information about Zania

Things we still need:

cash for the journey

soap

Walkman

bananas for the journey to the airport

important information about Zania

bus tickets to airport

envelopes to send letters home

first aid kit

video camera to record journey

cholera injection

D

TRIP TO ZANIA

To do

Supermarket – shampoo

Photoshop – video camera

Radio/TV shop – batteries

Things we still need:

dictionary: Zanian – English

traveller's cheques

cheese for the journey to the airport

mosquito repellent

some pens

find out about left-luggage facilities at the bus station

rucksack

railway information for Zania

UK embassy address in Zania

tetanus injection

5.2

Aim	
To complete a holiday questionnaire, then look for a compatible holiday companion	
Language	
Likes and dislikes	
Holiday vocabulary, e.g. *resort, excursion*	
Skills	
Reading and Speaking	
Lesson link	
Use after Unit 5, SB p52	
Materials	
One copy of the worksheet per student	

Pre-activity (10 minutes)

- Divide students into pairs and ask them to interview each other about their last holiday.

- Have a class feedback session and ask students to describe their partner's holiday.

Procedure (30 minutes)

- Explain that students have won the holiday of a lifetime. But there is one condition: they must go away with someone they have never met before! Their aim is to find a compatible holiday partner.

- Give each student a copy of the worksheet. Give students time to look at the worksheet and to check any items of vocabulary.

- Individually students complete the questionnaire. Tell students they can tick more than one option for some of the questions. For example, they may be interested in more than one destination, etc. Go around helping as necessary.

- Students mingle comparing their questionnaire answers in order to find a partner who has the same answers for at least six of the questions. When they have found a compatible holiday partner, students sit down. (As students start to pair off you may want to reduce the number of answers that they need to match to ensure that everybody finds a partner.)

- In their pairs, students now plan their holiday based on their areas of common interest. They must also negotiate any areas where there is disagreement to ensure that both partners will have a happy holiday. Go around listening and helping as necessary.

- Have a class feedback session. Ask students to tell the class about their holiday plans.

Extension (15 minutes)

- In pairs, students write a postcard from their holiday destination. Encourage students to say what the place is like and what they have done or are going to do.

- Display the postcards on the classroom wall. Give students time to read each other's postcards. Then hold a vote to see which pair is having the most interesting or unusual holiday!

holiday partners

holiday partners is a unique service for single people who are looking for the perfect holiday companion. Complete the questionnaire and we will find the right person for you. For each question you can tick more than one box.

We can take you anywhere!

1 What time of year do you want to go on holiday?
- [ ] Spring
- [ ] Summer
- [ ] Autumn
- [ ] Winter

2 What part of the world do you want to go to?
- [ ] Eastern Europe
- [ ] Western Europe
- [ ] Asia
- [ ] The Middle East
- [ ] Africa
- [ ] Australia / New Zealand
- [ ] North America
- [ ] South America

3 What kind of destination do you prefer?
- [ ] a beach resort
- [ ] a ski resort
- [ ] a large city
- [ ] a historic town
- [ ] a small village
- [ ] lakes and mountains
- [ ] other: _____

4 What do you like to do in the daytime?
- [ ] swim and sunbathe
- [ ] play sport
- [ ] go on organized trips
- [ ] explore local places
- [ ] go sightseeing
- [ ] go shopping
- [ ] other: _____

5 What do you like to do in the evenings?
- [ ] eat in a good restaurant
- [ ] relax in your hotel
- [ ] go to a bar/disco
- [ ] go for a walk
- [ ] go to a concert
- [ ] other: _____

6 Which statement(s) best describe you?
- [ ] I prefer to do things with my own friends.
- [ ] I like to make lots of new friends.
- [ ] I like to meet local people.
- [ ] I like to have some time on my own.

7 What accommodation do you prefer?
- [ ] luxury hotel
- [ ] budget hotel
- [ ] bed and breakfast
- [ ] self-catering apartment
- [ ] campsite
- [ ] youth hostel
- [ ] other: _____

8 How independent are you on holiday?
- [ ] I like to organize everything myself.
- [ ] I like organized activities with some free time.
- [ ] I like holidays with daytime and evening activities organized for me.

9 How much money do you normally spend on a holiday?
- [ ] £500 or less
- [ ] £500 to £1,000
- [ ] £1,000 to £1,500
- [ ] more than £1,500

5.3

Aim
To play a board game about travelling around the world
Language
Negotiating
going to and *will*
Skills
Speaking
Lesson link
Use after Unit 5, SB p52
Materials
One copy of the consequence cards cut up, one copy of the board game, a counter, and a dice per group of four students (If possible, enlarge the worksheets to A3 size)

Pre-activity (5 minutes)

- Brainstorm a variety of expression used for discussing options, making decisions and confirming decisions, e.g. *I think we should … , What will we do if …? What do you think? Yes, but if we do that, we will …? Perhaps we should … , OK, so we'll … ,* etc.

Procedure (30 minutes)

- Explain that students have planned a trip round the world and have estimated that it will take one hundred days. However, while on the trip things happen to them and depending on what they decide to do each time they will either save or lose time.

- Divide the students into groups of four and give each group a copy of the board game, one counter, and a dice. Keep the consequence cards for each group on your desk. (Make sure you organize the cards so that you can quickly find choice a, b, or c for a particular city when asked.) Give students time to look at the game and to check any items of vocabulary.

- Groups play by rolling the dice and moving the corresponding number of squares. Some squares simply require them to add or subtract days from their journey time (starting at 100), other squares require the group to make a decision. Ask each group to nominate a student to do the maths and to keep a running total of days.

- When the group lands on a square where they need to make a decision, one student comes to you and tells you their decision, e.g. *We're in Hong Kong and we've chosen option a). We're going to stay on for the competition.* Give the student the appropriate consequence card. The student takes the card back to the group, the group quickly reads it, adds/subtracts the required number of days to their journey time, and returns the card to your desk.

- When everybody has finished, have a class feedback session. Ask groups to tell you how many days they took to go round the world. The group who took the least time wins.

- If there is time, groups can play again, trying to improve on the decisions they made the first time.

Extension (15 minutes)

- In pairs, students write a series of postcards from the places where they had to make a decision, imagining they are writing to a friend explaining what has happened and what decision they are making. Go around helping with vocabulary as necessary.

Consequence cards

Beijing a	Beijing b	Beijing c
Sensible choice, but it takes ages to get your new passport. Add three days to your journey time!	The police tell you to try again a few days later – you do, but still nothing, so you have to go to the embassy anyway. Add seven days to your journey time!	They have your passport! Carry on and lose no time!

Hong Kong a	Hong Kong b	Hong Kong c
You have a great time and win second prize! You win enough money to take a plane instead of the train and catch up with your schedule. Save five days on your journey time!	You keep thinking 'What if I had tried?' The thought bothers you and you miss a train connection day-dreaming about it. Add a day to your journey time!	The police catch you trying to sell your ticket. You spend several days in the police station and have to pay a big fine. Add five days to your journey time!

Sydney a	Sydney b	Sydney c
It was hard to move, but you feel relaxed and look forward to new adventures with renewed energy. Lose no time!	You stay on, get more involved in the group and find it really hard to leave. You leave but feel very lonely and do nothing for over a week. Add nine days to your journey time!	You stay on, make good friends, fall in love, get married, and settle down for a long time. Go back to the beginning, adding all the days you have collected so far!

Delhi a	Delhi b	Delhi c
The doctor gives you some medicine and you feel better the next day. Lose no time!	You stay in bed for four days waiting to get better. You now feel better but you had a terrible time. Add four days to your journey time!	You push on but you feel worse and end up in hospital with a high fever. Add seven days to your journey time!

Madrid a	Madrid b	Madrid c
You go and think that it's one of the highlights of your trip. Then you meet a local who gives you a lift back to town. You lose no time after all!	You don't go, get on the train, then change your mind and go back. It's worth it but add two days to your journey time!	Nobody you ask has heard of it. You waste a day asking about it until you decide to go anyway. It is worth it but you add a day to your journey time!

Los Angeles a	Los Angeles b	Los Angeles c
You phone home but it takes you two days to persuade someone to lend you some money, and then another three days for the money to arrive. Add five days to your journey time!	You find a good job, meet lots of friends, and earn enough money to continue your journey in comfort. You can make up time by flying. Save seven days on your journey time!	One night your bag with all your money and your passport is stolen. It takes ages to get everything sorted out at the police and the embassy! Add fourteen days to your journey time!

Montreal a	Montreal b	Montreal c
You wait and the next day the strike is over. You enjoy your time and all you lose is a day. Add one day to your journey time!	There are hundreds of people hitchhiking and it's impossible to get a lift. You eventually arrive later than you expected. Add three days to your journey time!	The airport staff have gone on strike in sympathy with the railway workers. You already have the ticket so there's nothing to do but wait. Add four days to your journey time!

North Cape a	North Cape b	North Cape c
After a hundred kilometres the car breaks down. You go back to North Cape to have it repaired. Add ten days to your journey time!	The cycling is good, but very tiring. Halfway there you have to stop and rest. Add eight days to your journey time!	The reindeer is slow, but steady. It walks and walks, and you even learn to fall asleep while riding. Lose no time!

North Cape

There is no public transport for the next 2000 km to Stockholm. What do you do?

a   Buy an old car and hope to sell it later.

b   Cycle all the way.

c   A local has offered you a reindeer at a fairly cheap price.

Stockholm

You spend the day shopping for presents for all your family and friends. Add a day to your journey time!

Edinburgh

You see a special offer to go to Paris for only £10. You can't say no! Go back to Paris and add five days to your journey.

Round the world in a hundred days
START
London
FINISH

New York

Wow! There's too much to do. You have to stay longer. Add six days to your journey time!

Montreal

There is a rail and bus strike and you have to cancel your plans to go by train to the New York. What do you do?

a   Wait until the strike is over.

b   Try and hitchhike.

c   Catch a plane.

San Fransisco

You go back to Los Angeles to do more star-spotting in Beverly Hills. Add four days to your journey time!

Los Angeles

You're running short of money. What do you do?

a   Phone home and try to borrow some from your family.

b   Try to find a job locally.

c   Save money by sleeping in bus stations, railway stations, etc.

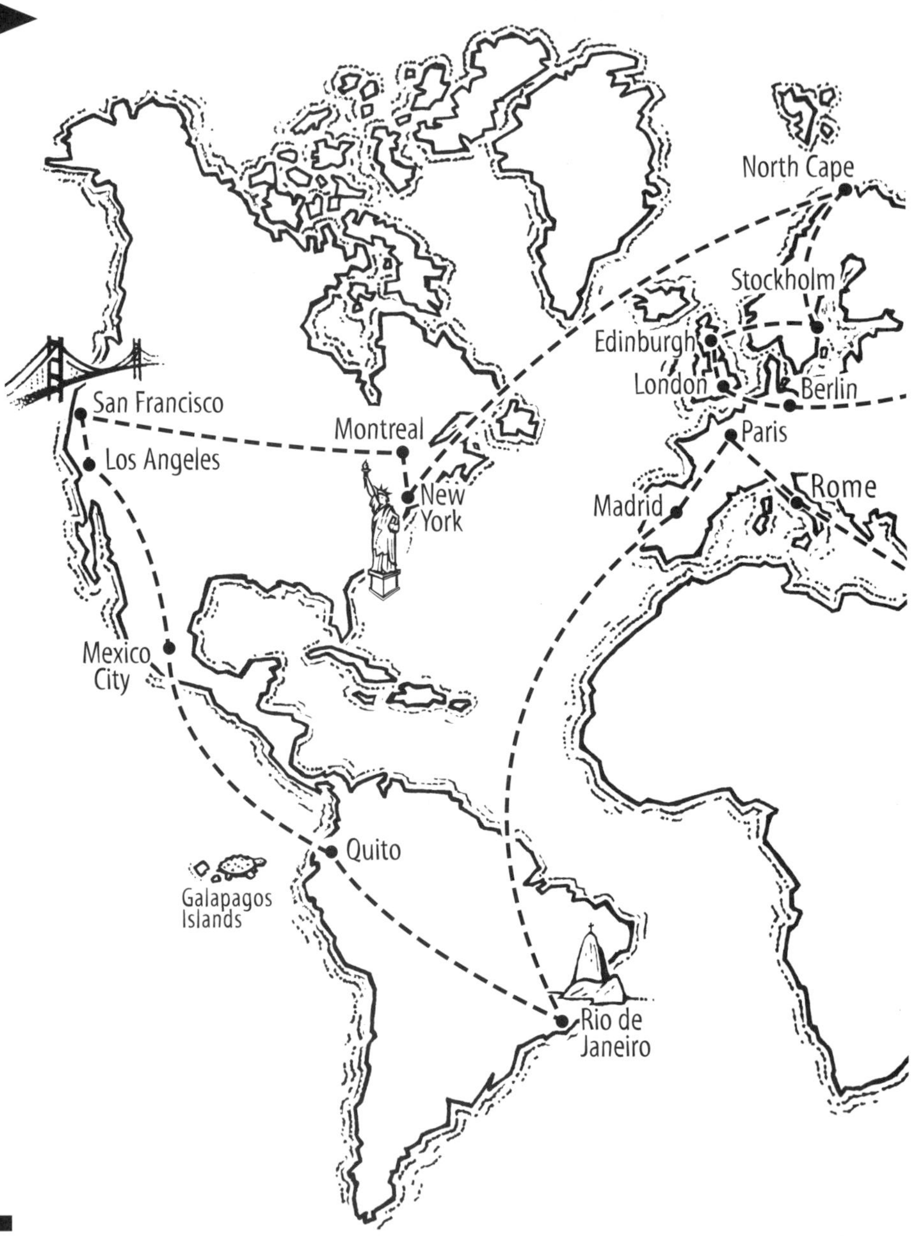

Mexico City

Things are going well. You like Mexico but you are getting tired from the heat. Move quickly on to Los Angeles and save two days on your journey time!

Quito

You decide you want to go to the Galapagos Islands and see the famous giant turtles. Add three days to your journey time!

Rio de Janeiro

You meet some friends travelling straight to Mexico city. Save three days on your journey time!

Madrid

A local resident suggests you go and see a fascinating historical site in the area, which isn't mentioned in your guidebook. What do you do?

a   Go anyway, it won't take long to get there.

b   Decide it's probably not worth it, if it isn't in your book.

c   Ask some other tourists if they know about it.

Map labels: North Cape, Stockholm, Edinburgh, London, Berlin, Paris, Rome, Madrid, San Francisco, Los Angeles, Montreal, New York, Mexico City, Quito, Galapagos Islands, Rio de Janeiro

Berlin

You've forgotten your traveller's cheques!

Go back to London and get them!

Moscow

You meet a rich businessman who gives you a lift in his private jet. Go to Tokyo and save two days on your journey time.

Beijing

After a night 'on the town' you find that you've lost your passport. What do you do?

a Go to your embassy.

b Go to the police station.

c Go back to the last bar you were in.

Tokyo

A fascinating city, but you resist all temptation to stay, so continue on your journey.

Hong Kong

You've entered a Karaoke competition! If you stay on two more days for the final competition you could win a large cash prize, but you'll miss your train and you've already bought the ticket. What do you do?

a Stay on for the competition and risk losing all your ticket money.

b Take your train as planned.

c Sell your ticket on the black market and stay on.

Sydney

The sun is shining, you've found a lovely place to stay, you meet a really nice group of people, but it's time for your next journey. What do you do?

a Leave as planned. You'll have to move on at some point anyway.

b Re-book your flight for a week later.

c Cancel your flight, lose some of your deposit, and stay on to see what happens.

Perth

InterPol contact you about a problem with your passport in Beijing. Go back to Beijing and add five days to your journey time!

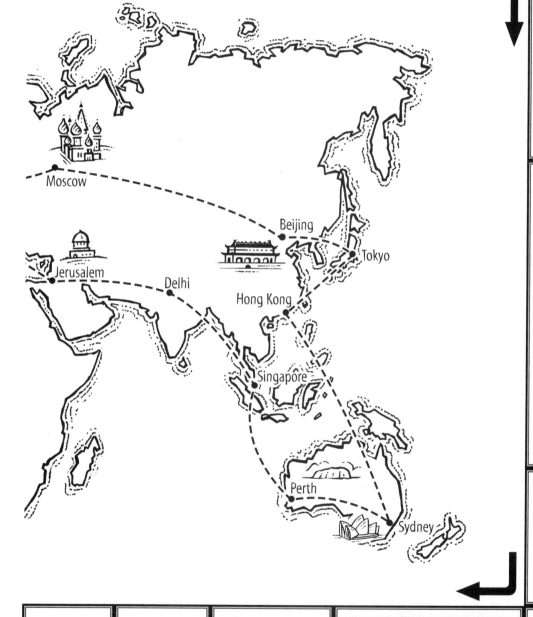

Paris

There's so much to see and do. You stay on longer. Add three days to your journey time!

Rome

Oh no! You catch the wrong plane! Add a day to your journey time!

Jerusalem

You're having an interesting time visiting all the famous sites. Everything goes according to plan and you leave on time.

Delhi

You've started to feel ill. What do you do?

a Go straight to the doctor.

b Stay in your hotel room and wait.

c Push on with your journey.

Singapore

You would like to stay longer, but you want to take advantage of special travel discounts. Go straight to Delhi and save two days on your journey time!

6.1

Our friend Ben

Aim
To find out what a mutual acquaintance was like at different times in his life

Language
Past Simple
Questions with *like*

Skills
Reading and Speaking

Lesson link
Use after Unit 6, SB p57

Materials
One copy of the worksheet cut up into cards per group of six students

Pre-activity (10 minutes)

- Write the following ages on the board: *15, 20, 25, 30, 35, 40*. Ask students what kind of life they think people lead at each age. Encourage them to talk about family life, work, problems, etc.

Procedure (30 minutes)

- Explain to the class that they all knew a man called Ben at different stages of his life and that they are going to tell each other what he was like when they knew him.

- Divide students into groups of six. Give Students A worksheet A, Students B worksheet B, and so on. Tell students not to show each other their worksheets. Give students time to read their worksheet and to check any items of vocabulary.

  Note: There are role cards for six students. However, this activity works equally well if you leave out Ian/Irene Wildegoose and Nancy Summerville.

- Ask students to think about how to answer the following questions about Ben for when they knew him.

  1 *How did I know Ben?*
  3 *What did he look like?*
  2 *What was he like?*
  4 *What did/didn't he like?*

- In their groups of six, students mingle telling each other about Ben. Encourage students to find out as much as they can about the life of Ben and to ask questions if necessary, e.g. *What did he look like? What was he like?* etc. Go around listening, helping and correcting as necessary.

- When everybody has finished, divide students into pairs to compare what they found out about Ben's life. Encourage students to think of reasons why his life turned out the way it did.

- Have a class feedback session.

Extension (15 minutes)

- Ask students, in pairs, to choose one point in Ben's life and write a diary extract for him. Go around helping with vocabulary as necessary.

A   Ian/Irene Wildegoose

You knew Ben when he was fifteen. You were his teacher!

Ben was a quiet student. He seemed to enjoy school and he was generally hardworking. He was also intelligent and he got high grades in nearly all of his subjects. He enjoyed sport and he was particularly interested in art and drama. You always expected he would continue to study one of these subjects at university, but then he got a place at Cambridge to study economics. In theory this was a great opportunity for him. After all, this would be the best way for him to get a good job. However, at the same time you thought that this decision had been forced upon him. Ben's parents were very domineering, which is probably the reason why he was so shy.

B   John/Jane Sparrow

You were at university with Ben in the early 80s. You both lived in the same halls of residence.

Ben was studying economics, but he was always more interested in your course (theatre studies). You both acted in several plays for the students' drama society. He was never very good as an actor, but he was always quick to understand the real meaning of the play.

Ben was a good friend, but he was never very reliable. He'd obviously led a sheltered childhood, and the freedom of living away from his parents went to his head. He nearly got expelled in the first year because of his poor exam results!

C   Nancy Summerville

You went out with Ben in the summer of 1986.

Ben was working as a junior accountant for a large firm in London. He was only twenty-five but his salary was enormous! Life was great! He was good fun to be with, he had lots of energy, and he was always looking for new adventures. He had an expensive flat, the latest car, the best clothes … and huge debts on his credit card!

However, after a while it all became too much. Ben never seemed to stop moving and he could also be very selfish. The most difficult thing was that you never felt that you got to know the 'real' Ben. It was almost as though he was playing a part in a play.

D   Mark/Mandy Fitzpatrick

Ben was your first boss when you joined Abacus International, *a large firm of accountants in London, in 1990.*

Ben was a good boss at the start. He was obviously under a lot of pressure, but he always had time to listen if you needed help. But then things started to change for the worse. His moods became unpredictable and he would shout at members of staff for no good reason. At the same time he started making mistakes himself, including one mistake that cost the company over £50,000 in legal fees.

Some people in the office started to say that he had personal problems and that he should be sacked. However, you didn't wait to find out because you took a job with another company.

E   Rodrigo/Rosalina de Sanches

Ben turned up at your beach bar in Brazil in the summer of 1995. He was backpacking around the world and he asked you for some seasonal work. You employed him as a waiter.

Ben was a good worker (unlike some of the other temporary staff!) and he quietly got on with the job. He was kind to the customers, but he never spoke about his personal life. You suspected that he had something to hide, but that didn't matter as long as he did the work and stayed away from the till!

Ben enjoyed the space and fresh air by the sea. He became very interested in surfing. On his days off he would usually go into the local town. He had a girlfriend there, although he never brought her to the bar.

F   Andrew/Alison Lewis

You are a theatre director and you first met Ben two years ago after he sent you a script for a new play. The play was called Lost Ambition. *It was a great success on Broadway and it was eventually turned into a Hollywood film!*

Ben is very down-to-earth about his success. He lives with his Brazilian wife and young daughter in an old farmhouse in Scotland. In the morning he writes, and in the afternoon he loves to walk in the mountains with his dog.

He's been offered several opportunities to work for large film studios in America, but he has always chosen to stay in his remote home. The last time you asked why he never seemed to care about fame and money, he said, 'Life's too short for that. I'm just happy to be doing something I really love.'

6.2

Aim	
To complete sentences from prompts, then compare the sentences in small groups	
Language	
Verb + -*ing* or infinitive	
Skills	
Writing and Speaking	
Lesson link	
Use after Unit 6, SB p58	
Materials	
One copy of the worksheet per student	

Pre-activity (10 minutes)

- Write the following sentence prompts on the board: *I like … , I would like … , I asked her …* . Elicit the question forms for the sentence prompts, e.g. *What do you like doing? What would you like to do? What did you ask her to do?* etc.

- Ask students, in pairs, to ask each other the questions and come up with five possible endings for each of the sentence prompts, e.g. *I like swimming in the sea. I would like to see that film. I asked her to lend me her phone,* etc. Go around listening, checking that students use the correct form of the second verb.

Procedure (20 minutes)

- Explain that students are going to complete sentences with true information about themselves.

- Give each student a copy of the worksheet. Ask students to complete the sentences. Go around helping as necessary.

- Now divide students into new groups of three to four. Tell students not to show each other their worksheets but to compare what they have written for each by asking each other questions, e.g. *What do you want to do one day? What have you never tried?* etc. Go around listening, helping and correcting as necessary.

- Have a class feedback session. Ask students to tell you anything interesting they found out about each other.

Extension (15 minutes)

- Complete the sentences as a class, changing the *I* to *We* and trying to find something that everyone agrees on. Ask a student to write the sentences on a large sheet of paper as the class completes them and put it up on the wall as a class profile.

All about me

Complete the sentences with true information for you.

One day, I want _____

I have never tried _____

I often forget _____

I love _____

Soon, I really must _____

I wish people would stop _____

_____

After class, I would like _____

When I was a child, I enjoyed _____

I hate _____

I would never refuse _____

I can't stand _____

Our teacher often tells _____

The last time I made a promise was when I promised _____

_____

I hope _____

Once, I helped _____

Now discuss your answers in small groups, e.g. *One day, I want to give up smoking.
What about you? What do you want to do?*

Photocopiable

6.3

Buying a house

<table>
<tr><td>**Aim**</td></tr>
</table>

Aim

To buy a house to suit a new lifestyle

Language

House vocabulary, e.g. *semi-detached, cottage*, etc.

Skills

Reading

Lesson link

Use after Unit 6, SB p63

Materials

One copy of *The cost of living* worksheet per pair of students. One copy of the house advertisements cut into cards

House prices			
A	£81,000	E	£78,000
B	£64,500	F	£122,000
C	£110,000	G	£90,000
D	£118,000	H	£68,000

Pre-activity (5 minutes)

- Ask students if they have ever imagined being somebody else. Ask them to tell you what they find so appealing about the other person, e.g. their job, where they live, their lifestyle, etc.

Procedure (20 minutes)

- Explain that students are going to choose a new identity and then buy a new house to suit their new lifestyle.

- Divide students into pairs and give each pair a copy of *The cost of living* worksheet. Make sure the *Income and costs* section is folded over and that students do not look at it. Ask students to work through the worksheet questions.

- When students have made their choices, ask them to look at the *Income and costs* section and calculate how much money they have available to buy their new house. While students are working, display the eight house advertisements in different areas of the classroom.

- When everybody is ready, ask students to look at the house advertisements and find the house they think would suit them. When they have chosen, they come to you and ask you how much the house is. If the house is out of their price bracket, tell them they can go back and change some of their decisions from *The cost of living* worksheet to free up more money, e.g. fewer cars or holidays abroad, etc. Tell them they cannot change their jobs or the number of children though.

- When everybody has chosen a house they can afford, write the price of each house on the advertisements. Give students time to look at the prices and check they got the best house possible for their money.

Extension (15 minutes)

- Ask students to write an advertisement to sell their ideal house. Go around helping with vocabulary as necessary.

The cost of living   *What kind of lifestyle do you want?*

1 Choose a new identity. What's your job? Choose from the list. Be realistic with your choice! Do you really want to be a company executive? Are you ready to work twelve hours a day, every day?

Actor	Company accountant	Hairdresser	Sales person
Advertising consultant	Company executive	Journalist	Shop assistant
Artist	Designer	Lawyer	Small business manager
Builder	Doctor	Nurse	Social worker
Civil servant	Fashion Model	Office administrator	Teacher
Clerk	Gardener	Programmer	Technical engineer

2 Now decide:

   a How many children do you have, or want to have?
   b Do you want to give your children a private education, or send them to state school?
   c Do you want to go on holidays mainly in your country, or mainly abroad?
   d How many cars do you want in your family?

3 Think about where you want to live; do you want to live in the city, with all facilities and entertainment near to hand, or in the countryside? Remember, houses in the city are usually more expensive!

4 Read the *Income and costs* section below and calculate how much money you have available to spend on your house according to your job and lifestyle choices.

5 Now go out and try and find the best house to suit your needs.

You can change your decisions about how much money you want to keep for other things. For example, if you planned to have two cars, you can decide to have only one and increase the amount of money for your house. But you can't change your job or the number of children you have.

Fold

Income and costs

1 Look for your job in the table. This is the amount of money you have available to buy your house.

£100,000	£130,000	£150,000	£170,000
Actor	Civil servant	Company accountant	Advertising consultant
Artist	Designer	Doctor	Company executive
Builder	Journalist	Fashion model	Lawyer
Clerk	Nurse	Programmer	
Gardener	Office administrator	Small business manager	
Hairdresser	Social worker	Sales person	
Shop assistant	Teacher	Technical engineer	

2 Now subtract the following from your available money:

   a Children: subtract £5,000 for each child you decided to have.
   b Education: subtract £10,000 per child if you chose private education.
   c Holidays: subtract a total of £5,000 if you chose holidays in your country, £10,000 if mainly abroad.
   d Cars: subtract £10,000 for each car you decided to have.

A stylish two-bedroom flat, ten minutes by underground from the city centre. A modern kitchen and bathroom, and living room with views over the city make this an ideal purchase either for a small family, or a business executive wishing to have all amenities right outside the front door.

A compact terraced house set in a quiet residential area just under an hour from the city centre. Two bedrooms, a living room/kitchen and a bathroom complete this perfect first-time buyer's house. This property is convenient for work and all amenities.

A spacious flat suitable for the whole family. This flat has three bedrooms, a large living room, a kitchen, and a bathroom. Conveniently situated near the town centre, it provides the family with easy access to all the amenities one can expect in a city.

A large detached family house situated within easy access to the town (twenty-five minutes). Three bedrooms, a large living room, a well-equipped kitchen, a bathroom, a garden, and a garage make up this stylish suburban house. Fifteen-minute drive from a large shopping centre for all the family's needs.

E

This charming country cottage with a large garden is set in wonderful countryside. A cosy living room with a fireplace is just what you need in the winter evenings, and its two double bedrooms both have views over open land.

F

A large Victorian house, situated just under an hour from the town. With five bedrooms, a large garden, two bathrooms, a good-sized kitchen, and a two-car garage, this house is ideally suited to a large family.

G

A lovely semi-detached house, located within easy access of the town (thirty minutes). Upstairs are two bedrooms and a bathroom, and downstairs a large kitchen and spacious living room. At the back of the house is a small garden and porch where one can relax after work.

H

This bungalow would make an ideal house for the first-time buyer. There are two bedrooms, a living room, a kitchen, a bathroom, and a small garden. It also has a garage. On the outskirts of town, it has easy access to the centre by road, taking no more than an hour.

7.1

Aim
To interview and select candidates for four jobs
Language
Present Perfect Simple
Past Simple
Skills
Speaking and Listening
Lesson link
Use after Unit 7, SB p65 & 66
Materials
One copy of the worksheet cut in half per eight students

Pre-activity (10 minutes)

- Introduce the topic of CVs to the students. Elicit on the board the basic categories for a standard CV, e.g. *Name and personal details, Education, Work experience, Other experience (e.g. voluntary work, travelled round the world), Other skills (e.g. languages, driving, playing the piano), Interests.*

- Ask students to write their CVs. Go around helping with vocabulary as necessary.

Procedure (30 minutes)

- Explain that students work for an employment agency. They are going to interview four candidates and choose who would be best suited to each of the four jobs they currently have on offer.

- Divide students into an even number of groups of four: A and B. (If necessary, make two groups of three.) Give Groups A worksheet A, and Groups B worksheet B. Give students time to read the job advertisements and to check any items of vocabulary.

- Ask groups to discuss what kind of skills and experience a person needs for each of the jobs, and to prepare questions for an interview. Each student in the group should take notes.

- When everybody is ready, ask one Group A to work with a Group B. Tell Group A that they are the interviewers, and Group B that they are the candidates. Each student from Group A interviews one student from Group B, taking notes about the student. The interviews should last about five minutes and be carried out simultaneously. Go around listening, helping and correcting as necessary.

- Then groups swap roles and repeat the procedure.

- When the interviews are finished, students, in their groups, compare their interview notes and try to allocate each student in the other group a job. Tell them they cannot give the same job to two people.

- When all discussions are finished, the two groups present their decisions. Have a class feedback. How many students are happy with their allocated job?

Extension (20 minutes)

- Ask students to write a job application letter for the job they were allocated. Go around helping with vocabulary as necessary.

A

Community Support Worker

Colchester County Services are looking for a Community Support worker. Duties include visiting and supporting vulnerable people living in their own homes.

You will be expected to work with people with physical, mental, or social problems, providing both practical and emotional support. You may be required to work some evenings and weekends.

SHOP MANAGER

Mood Fashion House is looking for a shop floor manager to supervise all aspects of its sales departments. You will be responsible for the design and layout of the shop, making sure they provide an attractive and pleasant shopping environment. After a period of training you will supervise the sales staff and take part in the selecting and buying of the clothes.

TRAINEE ASTRONAUT

Space Tours is seeking astronauts for its new Cosmo-holiday shuttle. You will be fully trained to pilot the shuttle, monitor the technical equipment, and carry out maintenance tasks. Trips will last for up to one month at a time, with two weeks' rest after each trip. A physically demanding job – applicants must have a high level of fitness.

ENTREPRENEUR

MobCom is an idea waiting to make a million. We have the idea, we need someone to make it work. Do you have what it takes to set up a new business, see it grow, and make it a success? We will provide you with some training in business skills and finance, but the desire to win must come from you! If you think you are the person we need, we want to hear from you now!

✂ --

B

Conference Organizer

Expo Millennium is seeking a person to take over the organization of conferences and seminars at their Head Office. You will be expected to arrange all aspects, including booking accommodation for visitors, communicating with international clients, preparing information and promotional brochures, organizing advertising and catering services. Some training will be provided.

Counsellor

A private health clinic is looking for someone to train as a counsellor. Your role will be to help clients cope with the difficulties in their life by talking, understanding, and leading them through a programme of confidence-building and personal development. The clinic also runs physical fitness courses as part of its programme, and a willingness to participate in these would be an advantage.

FILM DIRECTOR

ScreenMax is looking for a film director to produce exciting 21st century films for its new home entertainment Internet film service. The films are designed to appeal to the younger audience and be suitable to view on a personal computer. The work will involve directing the filming, editing and rewriting film scripts, and managing the special effects. Some training will be provided, but do you know what makes a film "buzz"?

School Director

UkanSpeak! is looking for a manager for its well-established language school in London. Your role will be to promote the school world-wide (so frequent travel will be necessary), recruit and select staff, and manage the school budget. Being able to teach a language would be useful, and you should be willing to help out with social events and summer excursions. We will provide the right person with the right training.

7.2

Snap!

Aim
To match passive sentences to the active equivalent

Language
Active and Passive

Skills
Reading and Listening

Lesson link
Use after Unit 7, SB p67

Materials
One copy of the worksheet cut up into cards per group of four students

Pre-activity (5 minutes)

- Ask students, in pairs, to write five sentences of different tenses and their passive equivalents, e.g. *They wash the dishes every day. The dishes are washed every day.* Go around helping and correcting as necessary.

- Combine pairs to make groups of four students. Pairs take it in turns to read out a sentence (active or passive) for the other pair to provide the active or passive equivalent.

Procedure (20 minutes)

- Explain that students are going to play snap by matching active and passive sentences which have the same meaning.

- Divide the students into groups of four and give each group a jumbled set of cards placed face down in a pile on the table, with the first card placed face up on the table.

- Students take it in turns to pick up a card and read it out slowly and clearly to the group. The other students listen and try to find a card that has the same meaning already on the table. If there is such a card, the first person to shout *Snap!* and place a hand on the card wins the pair. If there is no match, the student places the card face up on the table.

- The student reading the card cannot win the pair. However, if no-one notices a matching pair, he/she puts the card on the table and then claims the pair. (If a student shouts *Snap!* when the cards do not match, he/she must give back a pair he/she has already won by putting them back in the pile, and reshuffling the pile.) Go around listening, checking that students are playing correctly.

- Students play until there are no more cards. The student with the most pairs wins.

Extension (15 minutes)

- In their groups, students play Pelmanism with the cards. Groups mix up the cards and then place them face down on the table.

- Students take it in turns to turn over two cards, reading them aloud each time. If the cards match, the student keeps the pair. If not, the cards are turned over and the next student plays. Students play until there are no more cards. The student with the most pairs wins.

Mary woke John by shouting.

John was woken by Mary shouting.

John woke Mary by shouting.

Mary was woken by John shouting.

His father gave it to him.

It was given to him by his father.

He gave it to his father.

It was given to him by his son.

An accident caused the fire.

The fire was caused by an accident.

The fire caused an accident.

The accident was caused by a fire.

Ants ate almost everything.	Almost everything was eaten by ants.
Almost everything eats ants.	Ants are eaten by almost everything.
In one week, he's changed all his plans with her.	All his plans with her have been changed in one week.
She's changed all his plans in one week.	All his plans have been changed by her in one week.
Big fish catch little fish.	Little fish are caught by big fish.
Little fish catch big fish.	Big fish are caught by little fish.

Mary has left John.	John has been left by Mary.
John has left Mary.	Mary has been left by John.
The students have learnt a lot from the teacher.	The students have been taught a lot by the teacher.
The students have taught the teacher a lot.	The teacher has been taught a lot by the students.
Mary loves John.	John is loved by Mary.
John loves Mary.	Mary is loved by John.

7.3

Talk about yourself

Aim

To ask and discuss questions about personal experience

Language

Multi-word verbs, e.g. *put up with, take after, go out with*
Question forms

Skills

Speaking

Lesson link

Use after Unit 7, SB p72

Materials

One copy of the worksheet per pair of students

Pre-activity (15 minutes)

- Write these phrasal verbs on the board: *bring up, drop out, give up, turn out*. Check that students understand the meaning of each.

- Ask students, in pairs, to create a short life story for someone which includes the phrasal verbs. Go around helping with vocabulary as necessary.

- Have a class feedback session. Ask pairs to read out their stories to the class.

Procedure (20 minutes)

- Explain that students are going to interview each other about personal experience, e.g. a person they get on with, the last time they fell out with somebody, etc.

- Divide students into pairs and give each pair a copy of the worksheet. Read the conversation topics with the class and check that everyone understands.

- Ask students, in their pairs, to match the cartoons with the conversation topics. Then check the answers with the class.

- Explain that students are now going to interview each other about four of the conversation topics. Ask students, in their pairs, to choose the topics they would most like to discuss.

- Students interview each other. Encourage them to ask as many questions as possible. Go around listening, helping and correcting as necessary.

- Have a class feedback session. Invite students to tell the class anything interesting they found out about their partner.

Answers

1c 2i 3j 4d 5g 6h 7a 8f 9e 10b

Extension (20 minutes)

- Ask students to write a story that begins with the sentence: *Richard and Lara started going out with each other when they both worked in Tokyo.* Tell students to use the multi-word verbs in the worksheet in their story. Go around helping with vocabulary as necessary.

- Display all the stories on the classroom wall. Allow students time to read each other's work.

Talk about yourself

Match the cartoons with the conversation topics. Then choose four topics and discuss them with a partner.

1 ☐ a person you get on with very well

2 ☐ a person you take after

3 ☐ the last time you fell out with somebody

4 ☐ a person you used to go out with

5 ☐ something you are really looking forward to

6 ☐ something you hate but have to put up with

7 ☐ a bad experience that turned out well in the end

8 ☐ the last time you had to look after somebody

9 ☐ something you are putting off at the moment

10 ☐ something you have given up recently

8.1 Future scope

Aim
To discuss possible future inventions

Language
Second conditional

Skills
Speaking and Writing

Lesson link
Use after Unit 8, SB p78

Materials
One copy of the worksheet per group of three to four students

Possible sentences

1 If we could design babies, we could choose the colour of a baby's eyes.

2 If we had cars that ran on electricity, we could reduce world pollution.

3 If we lived to the age of 150, the world would become overpopulated.

4 If there were Trans-world express trains, we could go anywhere in the world for the weekend.

5 If drugs could improve a person's IQ, there would be no need to go to school.

6 If we could control the weather, we could make sure it never rained at the weekend.

7 If robots did the housework, we'd have no more arguments about doing the dishes.

8 If we could travel to other planets, we could take a holiday on Pluto.

Pre-activity (5 minutes)

- Ask students, in small groups, to think of inventions that are in common use today but which weren't generally available twenty years ago, e.g. *mobile phones, the Internet*, etc.

- Have a class feedback session.

Procedure (20 minutes)

- Explain that students are going to think of possible inventions in the future.

- Divide students into groups of three or four and give each group a copy of the worksheet. Explain that the eight pictures show possible inventions for the future.

- Ask students, in their groups, to discuss the eight pictures and together agree what each invention is. Go around listening, helping with vocabulary as necessary.

- Then ask groups to rank the inventions according to which they feel will become part of everyday life and which will always be science fiction.

- Have a class feedback session.

- Now ask students to think about how each of the inventions would change our lives if they were around today. Students discuss the consequences and write sentences, e.g. *If drugs could improve a person's IQ, there would be no need to go to school!*

- Have a class feedback session. Ask individual students to read out some of their sentences to the class. Allow time for other members of the class to ask questions.

Extension (10 minutes)

- Ask students, in small groups, to brainstorm ideas for a home of the future. Ask: *How would homes of the future be different with new technology? How would they be better places to live? How could technology change the following things: keys, telephones, shopping lists, door handles, household chores?* etc.

- Have a class feedback session.

FUTURE SCOPE

8.2

Strong adjectives crossword

Pre-activity (5 minutes)

- Do a quick drill of strong adjectives with the class. Ask: *Are you tired?* and encourage students to respond with a strong adjective: *Tired? I'm absolutely exhausted.* Continue with *good (fantastic), surprised (amazed)*, etc.

Procedure (20 minutes)

- Explain that students are going to work in pairs to complete a crossword puzzle with strong adjectives.

- Divide students into pairs. Give Students A worksheet A, and Students B worksheet B. Tell students not to show each other their crosswords. Give students time to look at their crossword, to check any items of vocabulary, and to prepare their definitions. Go around helping with vocabulary as necessary.

- Students work in pairs to complete the crossword by giving each other definitions for their missing words, e.g. *Number 2 is how you feel when you are very tired.* Encourage students to check the spelling and pronunciation if they are unsure. Go around listening, helping and correcting as necessary.

- Tell students that they can check their answers because the letters in the shaded boxes make a mystery strong adjective (*astonished*).

- Have a class feedback session.

Extension (10 minutes)

- Explain that students are on the last leg of a round-the-world trip. In pairs, students write a letter to a friend describing the trip and including as many of the strong adjectives from the crossword activity as possible. Go around helping with vocabulary as necessary.

A

1 A M A Z E D
2
3 F A N T A S T I C
4
5 E N O R M O U S
6
7 F A S C I N A T I N G
8
9 F R E E Z I N G
10

✂ ---

B

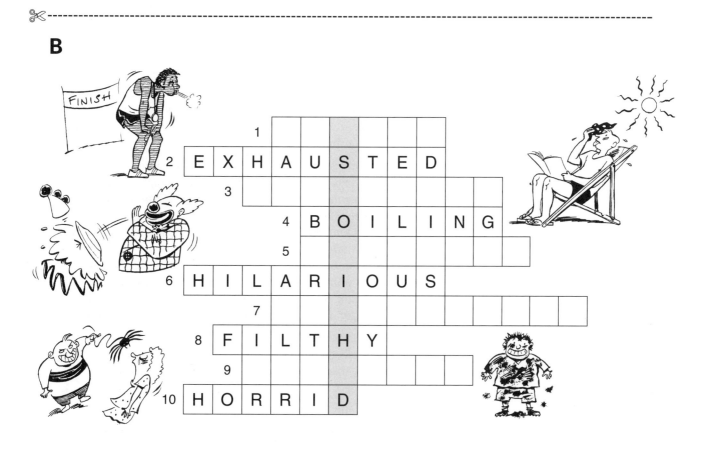

1
2 E X H A U S T E D
3
4 B O I L I N G
5
6 H I L A R I O U S
7
8 F I L T H Y
9
10 H O R R I D

9.1

Out of context

Aim

To deduce what a man is doing in different situations from his facial expression, gestures and posture

Language

Modal verbs of probability in the present, e.g. *must, could, might, can't*

Skills

Speaking and Listening

Lesson link

Use after Unit 9, SB p86

Materials

One copy of the worksheet cut up per group of four students

Pre-activity (5 minutes)

- To demonstrate the activity, hold up your hands in front of you as if you were driving a car. Ask students to tell you what they think you are doing, e.g. *You might be driving a car. You could be reading a book*, etc. Repeat with more obscure mimes to encourage students to use *could* and *might*, e.g. holding a hand close to your head (*You could be drying your hair. You might be speaking on the phone*, etc.).

Procedure (20 minutes)

- Explain that students are going to look at two sets of cartoons of the same man in a variety of situations. The first set are called *In context* because they show the complete scene for each cartoon, and the second set are called *Out of context* because they only show the man. His facial expressions, posture, position of hands, etc. in each cartoon are the same as the *In context* cartoons but there are no props, scenery, other people in the cartoon, etc. Students are going to each look at four *Out of context* cartoons and their accompanying clue cards and try to guess what the man is doing in each case.

- Divide students into pairs. Give Students A *In context* cartoons 1–4, *Out of context* cartoons 5–8, and *Clue cards* 1–4. Give Students B *In context* cartoons 5–8, *Out of context* cartoons 1–4, and *Clue cards* 5–8. Tell students not to show each other their cards. Give students time to look at their cards and to check any items of vocabulary.

- In their pairs, students take it in turns to talk about the cartoons. Student B tells Student A what he/she think might be happening in *Out of context* cartoon 1 using the modal verbs of deduction *must, could, might, can't*, e.g. *He might be looking at something. He must be on something because you can't stand like that normally*, etc. Then Student A reads out the clues on his/her *Clue card* for cartoon 1 for Student B to make his/her final guess about what the man is doing, e.g. *He must be playing pool for money against the other man.* Student A can tell Student B how close he/she was to the correct answer by showing him/her the *In context* cartoon.

- Then students swap roles and Student A tells Student B what he/she thinks the man is doing in one of his/her *Out of context* cartoons. Go around listening, helping as necessary.

Extension (10 minutes)

- In pairs, students create and mime an out-of-context scene for the class to guess what they are doing.

In context cards

Out of context cards

Clue cards

1

In this picture, I can see some money.

There's another man.

There's a table.

2

In this picture, I can see the sky.

There's a bridge.

The man is attached to a rope.

3

In this picture, the man is happy.

There's a book.

There's a weighing machine.

4

In this picture, I can see two chairs.

The man's wife is in the picture.

There's a small animal.

5

In this picture, the man is in pain.

There's another man.

They're sportsmen.

6

In this picture, the man is at home.

He isn't alone.

He's got two young children.

7

In this picture, it's important that the man is very quiet.

He's in a wild place.

There's a big animal.

8

In this picture, the man is kissing something.

He made it.

It moves very fast.

9.2

Whodunnit?

Aim

To deduce from clues who is most likely to have committed a crime

Language

Modal verbs of probability in the past

Skills

Reading, Speaking, and Listening

Lesson link

Use after Unit 9, SB p88 & 89

Materials

One copy of the worksheet cut up into cards per group of four students

Answer

There is no definite answer. The most likely candidate is probably Mr Y, although it is doubtful if he could have (and would have) travelled 15 km across London and then sat in a café half an hour after the robbery took place. Perhaps the witness made a mistake about seeing him in the café.

Mr T could have done it, but it is unlikely he would have had time to commit the robbery, get to Edinburgh the same day for a business meeting, and come back to London the following morning.

Mr X could have done it. The witnesses might have made a mistake and maybe the woman wasn't driving the car, but an unlikely mistake.

It couldn't have been Mr S because he's got a black car and is only 1.75 m tall.

Pre-activity (5 minutes)

- Introduce the topic of witnessing by asking students, in small groups, to describe one of the following:
  1 the first person they saw on leaving their home this morning
  2 the entrance to the school building
  3 what they were doing between 5.30 and 6.30 p.m. yesterday evening.
- Have a class feedback session. How good a memory for detail have students got?

Procedure (20 minutes)

- Explain that students were witnesses to a bank robbery and this is what they saw:
  The robbery took place on Monday at 9.30 a.m. at the Midwest Bank on Oxford Street, London. The bank robber was in his mid-thirties, tall, with dark brown hair. He was wearing a blue jacket and dark blue or possibly black trousers. He escaped in a blue Ford Mondeo car, which was parked outside the bank. The driver of the car was a woman in her mid-thirties with short fair hair. She was wearing sunglasses.

- Now tell the class that the police have some information about four suspects which they would like the witnesses to go through. Emphasise that these people are only suspects. Their task is to decide who is most likely to have committed the crime.

- Divide students into groups of four and give each group a set of information cards placed face down on the table.

- Students take it in turns to turn over a card, read the information about a suspect, then turn the card back over and remember the information. They then discuss whether this person could/couldn't have committed the crime, e.g. *He couldn't have done it because he was on a train at the time. He might have done it because he's got the same kind of car,* etc.

- When students have read all the information, they should decide who they think is the most likely suspect.

- Have a class feedback session. Does everybody agree?

Extension (15 minutes)

- Ask students, in pairs, to write a report to the police, stating who they think might have done it, who couldn't have done it, and why. Go around helping with vocabulary as necessary.

On Monday, Mr S was seen near the bank.	On Monday, Mr X was wearing a denim jacket.
Mr S owns a Ford Mondeo.	Mr X has got financial problems.
Mr S is 1.75 m tall.	Mr X admitted to being in the area between 9 and 10 a.m. on Monday.
Mr S has got a bank account at the Midwest Bank.	Mr X was seen driving off in a car with a female passenger.
Mr S has got a black car.	The woman in the car with Mr X was blonde and was wearing sunglasses.
Mr T is a semi-professional basketball player.	Mr Y is a student at London university.
Mr T works for a bank.	Mr Y has got a girlfriend with short, fair hair.
Mr T returned on Tuesday morning by train from a business trip to Edinburgh. (The journey takes five hours.)	Mr Y was wearing jeans and a blue coat on the day of the robbery.
On Sunday, Mr T was seen walking towards the bank with a woman who was wearing sunglasses.	Mr Y hasn't got a driving licence.
Mr T has got short, brown hair.	On Monday, Mr Y was seen at about 10 a.m. in a café 15 km away.

10.1

Aim
To match cards to make compound nouns

Language
Compound nouns

Skills
Speaking

Lesson link
Use after Unit 10, SB p103

Materials
One copy of the worksheet cut up into cards per pair of students: A and B. Keep the cards for each student separate and divide each student's cards into two groups; group 1 with the *A* (or *B*) on the left of the card, and group 2 with the *A* (or *B*) on the right

Pre-activity (10 minutes)

- Write the following words on the board: *alarm, rush, coffee, lunch, evening, night, sweet, clock, hour, break, time, meal, out, dreams.* Ask students, in pairs, to make six compound nouns and then order them to form a logical sequence throughout a normal day (*alarm clock, rush hour, coffee break, lunchtime, evening meal, night out, sweet dreams*).

Procedure (20 minutes)

- Explain that students are going to play Pelmanism where they match word cards to make compound nouns.

- Divide students into pairs. Give Students A a set of A word cards (in two groups), and Students B a set of B word cards (in two groups), placed face down on the table. Ask students to spread out their cards, keeping their two groups separate, so that each card can be seen.

- Give Students A the answer sheet for Student B, and give Students B the answer sheet for Student A. Tell students not to show each other their answer sheets.

- Students take turns to turn over a card from each of their group of cards. If the cards make a compound noun, the student invents a sentence with that compound noun. The other student checks the compound noun is correct by looking at the answer sheet.

- Students remove their cards after each correct answer and continue to play until the cards they turn over don't make a compound noun. Go around listening, helping and correcting as necessary.

- The first student to correctly match and remove all their compound nouns wins.

Extension (15 minutes)

- Ask students, in pairs, to write a story (100 words) including six of the compound nouns from the worksheet. Go around helping as necessary.

A	smoked	salmon	A
A	film	director	A
A	dining	room	A
A	football	pitch	A
A	book	case	A
A	detective	story	A
A	traveller's	cheque	A
A	business	trip	A
A	fire	work	A

A	sun	set	A
A	chocolate	cake	A
A	wine	bottle	A
B	tea	spoon	B
B	snow	storm	B
B	word	processor	B
B	food	poisoning	B
B	mobile	phone	B
B	life	story	B

B maternity	leave B
B air	conditioning B
B traffic	jam B
B travel	agent B
B back	ache B
B bank	account B

Answers for Student A's cards

smoked salmon
film director
dining room
football pitch
bookcase
detective story
traveller's cheque
business trip
firework
sunset
chocolate cake
wine bottle

Answers for Student B's cards

teaspoon
snowstorm
word processor
food poisoning
mobile phone
life story
maternity leave
air conditioning
traffic jam
travel agent
backache
bank account

10.2

Aim

To role play complaining about a hotel and some guests

Language

Complaining

Skills

Speaking

Lesson link

Use after Unit 10, SB p106

Materials

One copy of the worksheet cut in half per pair of students

Pre-activity (15 minutes)

- Introduce the topic of staying in a hotel by asking students to tell you about some of the places they have been to. Encourage students to give examples of things that could lead to complaints when staying in a hotel. Have your students got any real life horror stories?

Procedure (20 minutes)

- Explain that students are going to perform a role play where two holiday makers have complaints about a hotel, but the hotel owners feel that their complaints are either unjustified or completely misguided!

- Divide students into an even number of pairs: A (holiday makers) and 11B (hotel owners). Give Pair A worksheet A, and Pair B worksheet B. Ask students, in their pairs, to discuss what is happening in the pictures.

- Explain that the holiday makers are going to complain about everything shown in their pictures. The hotel owners are going to defend themselves according to the facts as seen in their pictures. Go around helping with vocabulary as necessary.

- When everybody is ready ask students to perform the role play. Encourage students to try to reach some kind of understanding rather than just having a terrible row! Go around listening, helping and correcting as necessary.

- Invite groups to act out their role play for the class.

Extension (20 minutes)

- Ask students, in pairs, to write a letter of complaint to a hotel owner or travel agent. Go around helping with vocabulary and ideas as necessary.

A You are Bob and Dorothy. You stayed in Will and Lucy's hotel and you had a terrible time! Look at the pictures and prepare to complain to Will and Lucy.

Bob and Dorothy

The building work

The swimming pool

The restaurant

The party

The price

B You are Will and Lucy. Bob and Dorothy stayed in your hotel. They're unhappy and have come to complain to you. Look at the pictures and prepare to defend yourselves.

Will and Lucy

The building work

The swimming pool

The restaurant

The party

The price

11.1

Kidnapped!

Aim

To role play a press conference

Language

Indirect questions

Skills

Speaking, Listening, and Writing

Lesson link

Use after Unit 11, SB p107

Materials

One copy of the worksheet cut in half per group of six students

Pre-activity (5 minutes)

- Ask students, in small groups, to think about the type of stories which make the front page of newspapers, both broadsheets and tabloids. Ask students to make a list of recent front page stories for each type of newspaper. Have a class feedback session.

Procedure (40 minutes)

- Explain that the king/queen was kidnapped recently but is now safely back at the palace. He/She is going to give a press conference and the students are journalists who are going to interview him/her.

- Divide the class into groups of about six students. Appoint the strongest student in each group as the king/queen, the others are journalists.

- Give a copy of the press release to the journalists. Give students time to read it and to check any items of vocabulary, and to prepare a list of about ten indirect questions to ask in order to get the full story.

- Meanwhile give each king/queen a copy of the full story. Tell them not to show it to the journalists. Ask them to read the story in preparation for answering the questions. (You may like to pair kings/queens during this reading phase.) Go around helping as necessary.

- When everyone is ready, ask each king/queen to sit facing his/her group of journalists. Tell journalists to ask as many questions as they can to get the story. Tell the kings/queens only to answer indirect questions and to make up details if necessary. Go around listening, helping and correcting as necessary.

- Stop the press conference after ten minutes, or when most of the questions have been asked. The journalists, on their own or in pairs, now write the story as a newspaper article. Set a strict fifteen-minute deadline. Meanwhile, the kings/queens, in pairs, write up the story as an interview to be printed in a magazine, including the questions from their press conferences. Go around helping with vocabulary as necessary.

- Display all the newspaper articles and interviews on the classroom wall. Allow students time to read each other's work and decide on the best interview and best article.

Extension (10 minutes)

- Students swap lists of indirect questions with students from other groups and re-word them as direct questions. Go around helping and correcting as necessary.

Press release for the journalists

Kidnapped!

The king/queen, whilst on a visit abroad, was kidnapped. A week later, his/her majesty turned up at four o'clock in the morning, at the mayor's house in a local village. He/She was wearing jeans and a T-shirt and was covered in dirt. His/Her majesty was in good spirits and health, apart from, rather strangely, badly-scratched knees.

✂ --

Full story for the king/queen

While you were overseas on an official visit, you were kidnapped by terrorists.

The kidnap happened while you were eating in your favourite restaurant, the Royal Piazza, which is owned by your brother. Several of the waiters suddenly took out guns and told your bodyguards to lie on the floor. The 'waiters' then blindfolded you and took you away by car.

When the terrorists finally took off your blindfold you nearly started laughing when you saw where you were. You recognized the inside of the building – it was the very same old castle that you used to play in when you were a child! The castle still belongs to your family, but nobody knows.

During your time in the castle, the terrorists were very nice to you, and you were given plenty of food and freedom. The terrorists did not want anything bad to happen to you because they knew it would be very bad publicity for them if anything went wrong. So you lived in the castle like, well, a king or queen! You

chatted to the guards, played chess with them, and generally relaxed. It was nice not to have to act like the head of a royal family for a while.

After a week, however, you began to feel bored and decided it was time to escape. You remembered from your childhood that there was a secret exit from the cellar, that evening, you told the terrorists wanted to go down to the cellar to see there was any interesting wine stored there. The terrorists thought this was a good idea and, because they thought there was no way out of the cellar, they let you go alone. After a while, you found the secret tunnel, and closing the door quietly behind you, you started down the tunnel. It was very small and often you had to crawl along on your hands and knees. You got very dirty! Finally though, you escaped and made your way to the next village and went to the mayor's house (all the mayors in the country were cousins, nephews or nieces of your family). He was very surprised to see you, and didn't recognize you at first because you were so dirty.

11.2

Aim
To match statements with question tags

Language
Question tags
Intonation

Skills
Reading and Speaking

Lesson link
Use after Unit 11, SB p109

Materials
One copy of the worksheet cut up into cards per group of four students

Pre-activity (10 minutes)

- Ask students, in pairs, to write five sentences of different tenses.
- When everybody is ready, ask students to swap sentences with another pair to supply the question tag for each. Go around helping and correcting as necessary.

Procedure (20 minutes)

- Explain that students are going to play Pelmanism with question tags. They have to match not only the correct question tags, but also the correct intonation: rising (↗) or falling (↘).
- Divide students into groups of four and give each group a jumbled set of cards placed face down on the table.
- Students take it in turns to turn over two cards, reading them aloud. If the two cards make a statement and the matching question tag with the correct intonation, the student keeps the pair. If not, the cards are turned back over and the next student plays. Go around listening, helping and correcting as necessary.
- Students play until there are no more cards. The student in each group with the most pairs wins.

Extension (10 minutes)

- Ask students, in small groups, to write more statements to go with each of the question tags, distinguishing between rising and falling intonation. Go around helping as necessary.

It's lovely weather,	isn't it?	↘
I'm not sure. Her name's Sandra,	isn't it?	↗
I saw you go red and smile when he spoke to you! You really like him,	don't you?	↘
Why don't you want to see him? I mean, you do like him,	don't you?	↗
I haven't seen you here before. You don't come very often,	do you?	↘
You don't know where I left my keys,	do you?	↗
That's a terrible result! You obviously haven't studied very hard,	have you?	↘
You haven't got any change for the coffee machine,	have you?	↗
Well, I suppose that's life. You can't always win,	can you?	↘
I really don't understand this. You can't spare a minute to help,	can you?	↗
You wouldn't do it even if I paid you,	would you?	↘
You wouldn't do me a favour,	would you?	↗

11.3

In my opinion

Aim
To take part in a debate

Language
Presenting opinions

Skills
Speaking

Lesson link
Use after Unit 11, SB p114

Materials
One copy of the worksheet cut up per class of sixteen students

Pre-activity (5 minutes)

* Write the following quotation on the board: *'No man is an island.' John Donne.* Ask students to first tell you what it means, and then say if they agree with the quotation. Encourage them to justify their reasons each time.

Procedure (20 minutes)

* Explain that students have been invited to talk on a variety of subjects at a debate.

* Divide students into groups of four: Pair A and Pair B. Give each group a different quotation. Give students time to read the quotation and to check any items of vocabulary.

* Tell students that they are going to debate their quotation. Pair A must argue in favour; Pair B must argue against.

* In pairs, students prepare their presentation. Encourage them to use the *for* and *against* phrases on page 114 of the *New Headway Intermediate* Student's Book. Go around helping with vocabulary and ideas as necessary.

* When everybody is ready, invite the first group up to the front of the class. Write the quotation they will be discussing on the board and make sure everybody understands. In turns, pairs give their presentations for or against the topic. Ask the class to vote on the presentation they found most persuasive. Continue until everyone has had an opportunity to present their case.

Extension (20 minutes)

* Ask students, in pairs, to write a newspaper review about one of the debates they heard. Go around helping with vocabulary as necessary.

'There is no such thing as society. There are individual men and women and there are families.'

Margaret Thatcher

'Health food makes me sick!'

Calvin Trillin

'Honest disagreement is often a good sign of progress.'

Mahatma Gandhi

'Sometimes I wonder if men and women really suit each other. Perhaps they should live next door and just visit now and then.'

Katharine Hepburn

'Technology is the knack of so arranging the world that we need not experience it.'

Max Frisch

'Happiness in intelligent people is the rarest thing I know.'

Ernest Hemingway

'The first half of our lives is ruined by our parents and the second half by our children.'

Clarence Darrow

'I cannot afford to waste my time making money.'

Jean Louis Agassiz

12.1

The bugged conversation

Aim

To prepare a radio report about a conversation between two criminals

Language

Reported speech
Reporting verbs, e.g. *beg, warn*

Skills

Reading, Writing, and Speaking

Lesson link

Use after Unit 12, SB p119

Materials

One copy of the worksheet cut in half per student

Pre-activity (15 minutes)

- Write the following reporting verbs on the board: *advise, tell, order, remind, beg, ask, invite, warn, refuse, offer.* Brainstorm situations where these verbs could be used, e.g. *A solicitor might advise his/her client to plead guilty.*

- Ask students to suggest what the person would actually say in each situation, e.g. *I think you should plead guilty.*

Procedure (30 minutes)

- Explain that students are going to write and deliver a radio news bulletin about a group of bank robbers.

- Divide students into groups of three and give each student a copy of the first part of the worksheet. Give students time to read the newspaper report that sets the scene and to check any items of vocabulary.

- Now explain that a cassette with a recording of a conversation between two of the robbers has been sent to the newsroom which proves that the gang is responsible for a recent robbery on the Central Bank of Barnsley. Tell students that their task is to report the details of the conversation in their news story.

- Give students a copy of the second part of the worksheet. This gives the transcript of the recording the newsroom received. Ask students to read the transcript and to discuss the following questions: *What is happening in the conversation? Where are the men? What has happened before? What happens next?* Then have a class feedback session.

- Write on the board: *A secret recording has led to the arrest of two members of the Johnson Gang.* Ask students, in their groups, to write a short news bulletin to follow this statement using reporting verbs to explain what was said and what happened. Encourage students to add more details to their stories to make them more interesting. Set a time limit of ten minutes. Go around helping and correcting as necessary.

- When everybody is ready, ask each group to nominate a newsreader to read out their news bulletin.

Extension (15 minutes)

- Ask students, in pairs, to discuss what they think actually happened and write a newspaper article. Go around helping with vocabulary as necessary.

- Display all the newspaper articles on the classroom wall. Allow students time to read each other's work.

Johnson Gang Strikes Again!

The notorious Johnson Gang is believed to be back at work after £1,000,000 was stolen in a raid on the Central Bank of Barnsley. The gang leader, Sid Crowbar, has not been seen since the robbery. Other members, including Tosh 'The Key' Smith and Arnie Thunder are also missing. Police have asked members of the public to telephone them with any information on 0281 623808. The investigation continues.

Sid Crowbar

Tosh 'The Key' Smith

Arnie Thunder

The Central Bank of Barnsley

TRANSCRIPT – Conversation between Sid Crowbar and Tosh Smith

Monday 2nd September

SID   Tosh, you're in big trouble!

TOSH   Please Sid, I put the money in the garage like you told me.

SID   Well, it's not there now! Where did you really hide it?

TOSH   Nowhere! I don't know where it is. Please let go, you're hurting me!

SID   I'll do a lot more if you don't tell me where you put it!

TOSH   What about Arnie? Remember, he's already left the country. I think he's taken the cash with him.

SID   Where's he gone?

TOSH   South America! You can call his wife if you don't believe me.

SID   I might just do that. But if you're telling lies, I'll be back to get you!

12.2

I'm really sorry!

Aim
To role play situations where an apology is required

Language
Apologizing and explaining

Skills
Reading, Speaking, and Listening

Lesson link
Use after Unit 12, SB p125

Materials
One copy of the worksheet cut up per group of eight students

Pre-activity (10 minutes)

- Ask students, in groups, to discuss the last time they apologized for doing something. Go around listening, helping as necessary.
- Have a class feedback session. Ask groups to tell the class the most interesting situations discussed.

Procedure (20 minutes)

- Explain that students have each caused an accident and have been the victim of a different accident. Students are going to mingle, explaining what happened to them and looking for and then apologizing to the person who was involved in the accident they caused.
- Divide the class into groups of up to eight students. Give each student a *Victim* card and a *Culprit* card. Make sure that the two cards are for different situations.
- Give students time to read their cards and to check any items of vocabulary. Encourage students to memorize the information but to keep the cards handy in case they need to refer to them.
- Students mingle in their groups and have one-to-one conversations taking it in turns to explain what happened to them (from their *Victim* card). If a student then finds that he/she is to blame for the accident (i.e. he/she has the *Culprit* card for that situation), he/she must own up and apologize. Then the student with the *Culprit* card gives the card to the student with the *Victim* card. Go around listening, helping as necessary.
- Students sit down when they have collected the *Culprit* card which matches their *Victim* card, and have also given away their own *Culprit* card to the correct victim.

Extension (15 minutes)

- Give each student a matching *culprit* and *victim* card and ask them to write a letter of apology to the person who suffered because of their actions. Go around helping with vocabulary as necessary.

A   VICTIM

Last year you lent a really good English dictionary to somebody in your class. You can't remember who it was, and they never returned it! You had to buy another one to study for your exams.

B   VICTIM

Last weekend you went to the beach. You went for a swim in the sea, but when you came out you noticed that someone had stolen your towel and clothes! You had to go home on the bus in your swimsuit!

C   VICTIM

You have just moved into a beautiful new home. However, when you got home from work yesterday evening the kitchen window was broken. There was a football inside, but nobody has owned up!

D   VICTIM

Last Sunday afternoon you were sitting peacefully in the garden. Suddenly a bag of sand fell out of the sky and hit you on the leg! You were in hospital for a week having operations on your badly-broken leg.

E   VICTIM

You flew home from a wonderful holiday last weekend. But problems started when you got to baggage reclaim in the airport. You waited for your suitcase . . . and waited . . . and waited! Eventually you were told that all the suitcases had been taken, including yours!

F   VICTIM

Last night you were woken up at 4 a.m. by loud banging on your front door. You went downstairs to see who it was, but there was nobody there! The noise had awoken your baby daughter, and you were awake with her for the rest of the night!

G   VICTIM

A few nights ago you were walking home. It was dark, but it was peaceful and you were happy. But suddenly you felt yourself falling, and you woke up half an hour later to find yourself in a hole in the road! Your ankle is still sore from the fall.

H   VICTIM

You started receiving junk mail about three months ago. The problem has become worse and worse, and now you are getting up to one hundred letters every day trying to sell you something!

A   CULPRIT

You have a terrible memory! For example, you borrowed a really expensive dictionary from a friend last year and you forgot to return it. You can't even remember who it belongs to now!

B   CULPRIT

Last weekend you went to the beach for a swim. You were in the sea for an hour, but then you realized you were late for a meeting. You ran out, got your clothes as quickly as you could and went straight to the meeting. But when you arrived you noticed that you had taken somebody else's clothes.

C   CULPRIT

You were playing football with some friends in the park. It was a great game until you kicked the ball really hard. It went over a garden fence and through somebody's kitchen window. You were so scared you ran away without saying sorry!

D   CULPRIT

Last Sunday you went for a ride in a hot-air balloon with a friend. Problems started when you began to fly low over some houses. You started to panic and released some sand bags to try and get more height. 'Not over houses!' your friend cried. But it was too late.

E   CULPRIT

You flew home from a holiday with your boyfriend/girlfriend last weekend. You had a row in baggage reclaim and you both got your suitcases and went home as quickly as possible. But when you arrived home you realized that you had taken somebody else's luggage!

F   CULPRIT

You had a terrible row with your girlfriend/boyfriend on the telephone last night. You were so angry you went round to her/his house and banged on the door very loudly. Then you realized that you were at the wrong house and you ran away.

G   CULPRIT

You're a road engineer. A few days ago you were digging a hole in the road when your wife called you to say she was in hospital because your baby was about to be born. You went straight to the hospital forgetting to put a safety barrier around the hole!

H   CULPRIT

You love to play practical jokes. A few months ago you read about a company you can contact if you want to receive lots of letters from other companies who are trying to sell things. You wrote to them and gave your friend's name and address.